Denizens of the Deep
true tales of deep-sea fishing

Books by Philip Wylie

Heavy Laden
Babes and Sucklings
Gladiator
The Murderer Invisible
Footprint of Cinderella
The Savage Gentleman
Finnley Wren: His Notions and Opinions
As They Reveled
Too Much of Everything
An April Afternoon
The Big Ones Get Away
Salt Water Daffy
The Other Horseman
Generation of Vipers
Corpses at Indian Stones
Fish and Tin Fish
Night Unto Night
An Essay on Morals
Crunch and Des: Stories of Florida Fishing
Opus 21
The Disappearance
Three to Be Read
Denizens of the Deep

and by Philip Wylie and William W. Muir
The Army Way

Denizens of the Deep

true tales of deep-sea fishing

by Philip Wylie

foreword

by Frank Sargeant

Skyhorse Publishing

Skyhorse Publishing books may be purchased in bulk at special discounts for sales promotion, corporate gifts, fund-raising, or educational purposes. Special editions can also be created to specifications. For details, contact the Special Sales Department, Skyhorse Publishing, 307 West 36th Street, 11th Floor, New York, NY 10018 or info@skyhorsepublishing.com.

Skyhorse® and Skyhorse Publishing® are registered trademarks of Skyhorse Publishing, Inc.®, a Delaware corporation.

Visit our website at www.skyhorsepublishing.com.

10 9 8 7 6 5 4 3 2 1

Library of Congress Cataloging-in-Publication Data is available on file.

Cover design by Jane Sheppard

Print ISBN: 978-1-63450-248-1
Ebook ISBN: 978-1-63450-890-2

Printed in the United States of America

Contents

this book is fondly dedicated
to two of the finest friends I have
who happen to be
two of the world's finest anglers,
Helen and Mike Lerner

Foreword: an outdoor writer's outdoor writer

If you know of Philip Wylie only as an old-time fishing writer, there's much to learn. He was emphatically not an "outdoor writer," in the sense that I, for example, am an outdoor writer. He was an actual, legitimate writer, who happened sometimes to write about fishing, simply because he loved it so.

His output included hundreds of mainstream articles, novels, serials, short stories, syndicated newspaper columns, and lots more. He also wrote screenplays while in Hollywood, was an editor for Farrar & Rinehart, served on the Dade County, Florida Defense Council, was a director of the Lerner Marine Laboratory, and at one time was an adviser to the chairman of the Joint Congressional Committee for Atomic Energy, which led to the creation of the Atomic Energy Commission, according to his bio in Wikipedia.

But you would never know any of this from reading his fishing stories—he simply sets his angling life aside from all the rest, and writes like one of the guys.

Writers are an envious bunch. One of the ways I can tell if a thing is well written is that somewhere in the midst of it I will find myself thinking, "Damn, I wish I had written that!" With Philip Wylie, there are those moments on pretty much every page. He is an outdoor writer's outdoor writer, a guy with wit, broad experience, and an obvious bone-deep knowledge of the fishing he writes about, and yet there's none of the elitist tone in his writing that seemed to creep into a lot of stuff written in his era, particularly among big game fishermen. He writes like a guy whom you might have shared a boat and a beer with last week. Wylie's stories were written, however, in the days when you could book an offshore charter boat and skipper for sixty-five to a hundred dollars per day, according to Wylie, who found it excruciatingly expensive.

Wylie is loaded with smart-aleck remarks that could have come from Dave Barry a few years back instead of a guy writing in the Eisenhower era. Like this: "Guys who buy a boat to save money on fishing are like those who marry their blondes [mistresses] to save money on jewelry."

And this: "Every metal part on a boat 'reacts' in sun, saltwater, and air. And here, by 'reacts' I mean 'falls apart in.'"

He talks thus about taking on really big fish, like tuna and marlin:

"At some point in the Homeric struggle, there is always a point . . . when the angler realizes . . . that he has set himself to do, *for fun*, something not unlike unloading a coal barge, alone, with a big shovel, fast—and no time even for wiping sweat."

Wylie was also one of the first to write about the then-infant sport of flats fishing for snook, sea trout, reds, mangrove snapper, barracuda, baby tarpon, and the like. And he had the sense of what it could become—lots of exciting fish easy to catch on light, manageable, and affordable tackle, many even catchable without using a boat but by wading or fishing from a bridge or pier, and not requiring the shoveling of the coal barge, either, when one was hooked.

To him every day on the water was a blessing, and he had many after he moved to Florida. "I haven't years enough, energy enough, or money enough to go on high adventures," he wrote in this book of his latter years. "I merely have high adventures where I am."

How can you beat that philosophy?

He was a friend of Hemingway and a force behind the founding of the IGFA with Michael Lerner. He lived in a day when "millions" of giant bluefin tuna went past Bimini in season, followed by a whole lot of very large mako and white sharks. He was evidently one of the few early on who appreciated sharks as a fascinating part of the sea's web, in an age when most anglers routinely killed every one they could lay hands on.

Sailfish, on the other hand, Wylie and apparently everybody else routinely brought on board and clubbed to death, at least early in his offshore career, an act that would horrify most billfish anglers these days. He fished them on 18-pound test braided nylon, and with the reels of that time, it must have been a tricky proposition. He began to release them, as he did all other species not taken for the table, as he gained experience.

"The angler . . . if he has the time to spend . . . in the end becomes less angler and more naturalist," he mused.

Simply read through the preface of this book and you're likely to wish you could have known Philip Wylie and shared a boat with him. Read the rest of the book and you're likely to feel you have. It's a voyage well worth taking.

Frank Sargeant was long time outdoor editor of the Tampa Tribune *and a senior editor of* Florida Sportsman Magazine *before he "retired" to work seventy hours a week at freelancing.*

Preface: *some thoughts on fishing*

In looking over the informal essays you are about to read —a collection arranged by my publishers—I felt that the net effect might, in some ways, be misleading.

For instance, fish aren't quite as easy to catch as it occasionally appears here. And the big ones in the sea aren't quite as accessible to the average Joe as he might imagine from reading this. It costs money and takes time to go after them, although sea fishing isn't exclusively a rich man's sport.

I would not want my readers to imagine that I, for example, had ceaselessly fared forth on the Gulf Stream and come in with the cruiser half sunk by its load of fish. And so, to correct such possible inference, I felt a Preface advisable—a note, let us say, of caution, coupled with a certain amount of confession of the sort said to be good for the soul. To wit:

In twenty-odd years of marine angling, in hundreds of days spent trolling on the sea, I have caught exactly two big bluefin tunas. I have never caught an Allison tuna, a mako, a broadbill swordfish. In a thousand hours of trolling for blue marlin, I have boated two. During that period, of course, I "hung" many more. Say twenty. I fought them—and lost them.

On the other hand, you are going to see that I am widely regarded as one who fishes under a spell, an evil spell. For I have lost a great many big fish under circumstances which have caused strong men to break down, dithering with wrath and impotence. I am supposed to be fairly competent as an angler. I have been selected to fish in tournaments, on teams, representing my club—a thing no dub would be chosen to do. So, you see, it is a matter of foul fortune, not skill, that attends my many failures. Anyhow, that's what I claim.

Let me explain the sort of Kismet (doom, I mean) that pursues me:

Some years back, I took dead aim at this problem. I decided to put an end to "Wylie's blight." I went about it modestly, selecting bass as my goal: I would build my own pond, raise my own bass in it, and then—by Triton!—*catch* a few!

Well, the pond was built in my mother-in-law's back acres. Bulldozers scraped deep into a miniature valley and raised up a dam at its end. The winter rains and snows filled the basin with water. That first year, it leaked. Undaunted, I re-bulldozed. The next year, the Conservation people came—and stocked it. Thereafter, patiently, I fertilized the pond—and my fish waxed fat and energetic. Cattails grew. Frogs croaked around the perimeter; willows rose and bent gracefully over the millpond green water; turtles turtled all day long, and by night the surface seethed with bass taking insects. Big bass, at last, edible and hungry, themselves. Still I waited.

Let them grow.

At length the great day came. I decided to chance nothing. No trout rod, no flies, for me. I had my own fish here, in my private rain barrel, and I was going to break my jinx by actually knocking them off like bowling pins. So I used worms, my friends. I fished all day in the rain—and I caught one bluegill.

What can you do about a thing like that? Sure. There was a reason. There is *always* a "reason." In this case, I figured it out—being an angler who understands better than nearly any other angler alive why it is you *don't* catch 'em. It seems that there was about the largest crop of tadpoles in that pond in the history of batrachians. There were so many tadpoles that, if you scooped up a bucket of water, it looked like tapioca. My fish had no interest in worms. They had plenty to eat. In fact, they probably had trouble *not* eating, because every time they drew an aquatic breath they must have sucked in ten tadpoles. The bluegill I did catch was the fattest bluegill I'd ever seen— he had actual chunks of fat inside him.

That's the sort of thing I'm up against.

You ought to know about it. You might run into it yourself. Or something like it.

There are other booby traps, hundreds, in angling.

In the case of lion hunting, I understand, the guide knows where lions live. You get in a veldtmobile (a word I just discovered) and the guide drives. He conducts you to some lion-infested purlieus and the lions look up as you step from the car. Leaning against a fender, you take dead aim, and kill one or two.

Not long ago, in an account of *rhinoceros* hunting, given by my friend Robert Ruark (who is an honest man), they went in a *station wagon*. They located dozens of rhinos, but never one to suit. To shoot, that is. Some had horns that were too small and some were personally runty and some were the wrong sex. They loitered around all day in the midst of this rhino-swarm and Bob read a mystery story while he waited for the exact rhino to come along. It never did, which is the only thing about his tale that surprised me.

Going after big fish is nothing like that. Nothing whatever, even if you discount the difference between a boat and a veldtmobile. There *is* a difference, even there, too! Bob said the bumpy rides into the eland country (or maybe it was the gnu country) made Mrs. Ruark uncomfortable. Well, Mrs. Ruark ought to see how it feels to spend a day on a thirty-two-foot cruiser in a forty-mile wind blowing against the current of the Gulf Stream! The Ruarks said it was mighty hot in Africa, also. I will give them ten degrees and bet even, on the cockpit of a fishing boat hard by the Tropic of Cancer, in mid-July, on a cloudless noon when no breeze is blowing. We tropical fishermen don't think it's warm unless the brightwork sizzles when you spit on it, and the skipper makes toast on the forward hatch-cover. Well, almost.

Then, fishing guides don't even know where marlin live. Nobody knows. A tiger or an elephant is a fairly local species. You can follow your beaters into a certain valley in the full assurance that, right in the high grass ahead there are water buffalo and, for heaven's sake, *look out!* Hunters have what they call "signs" to go by. Signs like footprints, for instance. But tuna leave no tracks even though some of them do seem to travel the same seaways at approximately the same time every year. On the whole there is mighty little "sign" for fish.

People say, of course, that a passel of hovering birds is sure evidence of fish. But I have personally investigated the sea beneath 1,365,854 flocks of birds, ranging from pelicans to plovers, and all I usually found there was the garbage just dumped by a passing freighter. Off and on, for most of my adult life, I've looked for marlin sign, too—and I spotted it only *once*. It happened off the Florida Keys and the "sign" was the sight, here and there, of mackerel with broken backs flopping on the surface. From this we inferred that marlin were swatting at mackerel schools, and we were apparently correct because we hung two marlin that day. But this "sign" had never been seen before by our guides and they have never seen it again, that I know of. Bear sign isn't that scarce.

When you hunt for big fish you just hunt blind. No way to tell where they "are," usually. For all you know, they may be right there under your baits—a half mile down, in the dark—not seeing a damned thing or interested in top-water food. If giraffes had wings and spent a good deal of time soaring near the stratosphere, that would make the finding of giraffes like the finding of, say, a broadbill.

All your fishing guide does know for sure is that, in past years, somebody or other did catch a fish of the species you seek, somewhere in the neighborhood of the spot where you're trolling. If lions spent some of the time in Africa and some of the time in Poland, lion hunting would be more like fishing. For you can leave your home in Baltimore, say, and travel to Miami—one thousand lousy miles and more—and fish for a week for white marlin and never get a strike. Then you can come home and discover they've been catching white marlin like herring, right off Ocean City, Maryland. Things like that make guiding tough. They make fishing tough.

I won't carry the analogue much further for fear of making certain kinds of big-game hunters look sissy. But I guess you get the idea. Put it this way: When a hunter goes to Africa for a few weeks of shooting, he always comes back with enough "heads" to make his den look like a petrified zoo. But when a big-game angler goes big-game fishing for a few weeks, he often comes back with a sunburn, and nothing else.

However, even one big-game fish puts the angler in a special league. Catching one is something like having appendicitis. You will notice that a person who has had an appendix operation talks about it with authority. He talks authoritatively about *all* appendix operations. In fact, gradually, he becomes a lay authority on general *surgery*. This also happens to anglers. Let a mere man or woman nail a blue marlin, or even an outsized white marlin, and you will thereafter find yourself, whenever that person's around, in the presence of an all-round big-game angler.

Besides, if you fish a good deal, even though you don't catch many, you'll *see* some caught. You can talk about that.

In my own case, I've sat for hours—maybe a little listlessly at times—while some of the largest fish in the world were taken by my guests. Any experience missed by me has been directly observed by me. Let that stand as an answer to those several skeptics who, upon reading the *fiction* I have written about deep-sea angling, wrote to say they thought I'd never fished at all. That's what I've done most of—*fish; not catch* fish.

The essays ahead are factual. They concern data known to me; they contain accounts of events that happened to me or in my presence; and they also report fishing anecdotes collected by me from credible sources. So far as I am aware, there is no "fiction" in this book. However, since fishermen appear to be the sports world's stickiest people about detail, let me say that even when a writer composes fishing fiction, he is held strictly accountable to fact. Nothing must happen in a story that could not take place in reality.

Once, just once in the hundred or more yarns I've written about deep-sea fishing, I described a certain fish—a permit, actually—as having a "streaming" dorsal fin.

Well, a permit is a pompano and I was thinking absently of an African pompano which, it happens, does have a set of dorsal streamers. But you would think I had attributed the Gettysburg Address to Washington! Letters poured in. My phone sang day and night. I was corrected by ichthyologists, small boys, fishmongers and maiden aunts. I hadn't believed there were that many people in U.S.A. who'd ever even *heard* of permits!

This circumstance applies, in some nth power, to the essay on angling. In fact (and this is a bee I trust the reader will get firmly in his fly-hat) I am continually "corrected" by people who have *mistaken* information; they plough into the mill-pond of my life to controvert some proper assertion. Be it noted here, then, that all such communications will be folded neatly and used (unanswered) to clean reels, prop up tables, and the like. Let me illustrate this monkeyshine:

In a piece appearing here—about sharks—I point out that these beasts rarely attack human beings and may be driven off, frequently, by determined counterattack. Is that clear? Go back and study it. Very well.

When that assertion was published in what is usually called "a national periodical" (and what we here shall call *True* magazine), a tragedy occurred off California. Two teen-age boys, in swimming, were attacked by a shark. One was bitten so badly he bled to death. The other, trying to help his pal, slugged the shark with his fist and drove it away. Now, tens of millions of man-day swims occur annually off California and that instance of shark attack was the first recorded on the entire coast for more than eleven years.

Clear enough, isn't it? Observe from it that sharks rarely attack people off California and the only one that did so, in eleven years, was driven off by a sock with a bare fist. He was even driven off *after* he'd had one big bite of a person.

There could hardly be a more convincing proof of my

argument about the rarity of shark bite, the possibility of defense.

But what happened?

For days, for weeks, for *months,* my mail contained scurrilous letters from people who tore out my article and the tragic news clipping, pinned them together, and scribbled to me, "Guess this makes you feel like a horse's neck!" (Note: Horse's neck was about the mildest expression these oafs used!)

I have turned this matter over to some of my friends who happen to be psychoanalysts. I have pointed out, in doing so, that my article *also* said (look for yourself) that once in a great while sharks do kill people and quite often the Australian sharks try it. The psychoanalysts are still pondering the problem of how it happens that people will mail you *proof of something you wrote,* in the imbecile belief that it proves the *opposite!*

"People don't think," one learned man hazarded, "when confronted with anything that scares hell out of them. Look at McCarthyism," this sage mused. "Separates the men from the boys, the sane from the hysterical."

Well, you look at McCarthyism.

Take Portuguese men-of-war.

These are the very handsome relatives of the jellyfish that float around with their opalescent-blue gasbags inflated and their long, barbed streamers hanging in the water. They are poisonous. Some people are more sensitive to the toxin on their trailing stinging-cells than others. But suppose you gather a group of innocent people and divide them in half. Tell one half that the Portuguese man-of-war causes a burning sensation that doesn't seriously distress most persons and can be relieved by an alkaline application. Tell the other half that the same critter is capable of inflicting "agonizing" harm on people and some people have even been killed by the monster. (Both statements are true.)

Now. Put these people in swimming along Miami Beach on a day when the men-of-war are around and the wind's east. Let all these Joes and Jills get tangled with the sea varmints. You will find, I am sure, that the people who expected to be half-killed get in a prodigious uproar; those who merely expected the kind of burn you get from nettles will hold up dandy—probably go right on swimming, as myriads do. But I've seen people—preconditioned people—sent to the hospital for men-of-war "agony."

What, you may ask, has all this to do with McCarthy?

What, I ask you in return, has he got to do with fishing?

I have mentioned *cost*. A great many deep-sea anglers have said a great deal about cost. Said it with sorrow.

In order to fish in the open ocean, one needs a substantial boat: the waves get big. One needs a motor: you can't row fast enough to troll for sailfish. A motor alone needs a biggish boat —and somebody to run it. That means a boatman. If you aren't very familiar with deep-sea fishing, you also need guidance. And, anyway, if you catch a really big fish, you'll need help getting him aboard. It adds up—adds up, these days, to an average cost of sixty-five to a hundred dollars a day, for a charterboat.

If you take three paying people along, that sum comes down to a manageable amount, for a day's gamble. You spend more at a race track—and get even less. But suppose the people you take along are (a) your wife and (b) your parents-in-law. This means you pay the full freight. Sixty-five simoleons, at least. Can you afford it?

Many people have answered that question in what seems to me the most uneconomic (not to say crazy) fashion imaginable. *They have bought their own boats.* Now, I will not argue with a person who "loves" boats and buys a boat because he loves boats, any more than I would argue with a man about the cost of a bracelet he gave to a girl, owing to his love of blondes. People are entitled to such whims. This is (or was) a free country. Every man is allowed to think as he pleases, excepting when a bully from Wisconsin disagrees. What I mean is, people are still allowed to love boats, as this Preface goes to press.

But the men who buy boats because "they want to save money when fishing," are marrying their blondes. If you have a boat, you have to buy a dock, or rent one. Then you have to hire a full-time man to run your yacht—unless you are willing to give up fishing and become a sea-chauffeur for your pals. You may also hire a mate to bait and to boat fish while your hired captain steers. Now you have a boat, a dock and two personnel on your payroll. You think that's anything? You aren't even in the water, yet!

You have to get the damned thing to the sea and into it, probably paying for the use of ways, trucks, whatnot. And when it hits the water, you really begin to spend money.

I have nothing against boat-makers, personally. I know some, clean-shaven Detroit millionaires, and no wonder. The only thing I demur at, in boat-makers as a class, is their illusion. They somehow imagine they have mastered the art of boat-making. Nothing could be farther from the fact.

For there is no substance in or on or under or around a boat that they have learned to do a good job on yet—and they've been at it since Noah. For instance, every metal part on a boat "reacts" to sun, salt water and air. Here the phrase "reacts to" means "falls apart in." Most metal, in fact, rusts, corrodes or oxidizes faster than the human hand can polish. Wood in sea water is just borer-bait and sea-garden soil. Zillions of plants and animals take up residence on and in your hull, and unless you are a marine biologist, this booteth you naught. When your boat gets much of this stuff in and on it, you have to haul it out of the water, scrape it and paint it. When the accumulation gets really sinister, you have to abandon ship because it isn't "seaworthy" any longer.

Furthermore, what happens to paint, varnish and plastics on boats, should give nightmares to the du Ponts. All in all, when you consider those costs, and then realize a fishing guide will take you out for maybe sixty-five a day, mate thrown in, you wonder what charterboatmen's families eat. Put it this way:

Years back, I used to fish on charterboats a hundred days per annum, approximately. And I figured even that cost represented a saving of 50 per cent on an owned boat. It also freed me to fish the whole time and it excused me from trying to explain why I couldn't fix what had busted every time the Coast Guard towed us in.

Here I shall give you a tip worth the price of this book a hundred times over:

Charterboatmen, as a group, run constantly, and they understand boats; they always take you out and get you back safely. That has been my experience. *But so-called "private" boats break down.* They usually break down on the way out, about at the mid-point between home and the fishing grounds, over a mudbank where there's a nasty ground swell and you can't catch a flounder on a golden hook. This last is important because when private boats break down, you usually have to spend a lot of hours just *being* there. So you fish—in the wrong spot. Some people have been obliged to spend *years* after being marooned by boat-fault. The Florida Keys are partly populated by the descendants of such shipwrecked persons; so are various islands in the Indian Ocean. By and large, then, stay off private boats if you expect to fish much.

Of course, on charterboats the tackle is supplied.

But for those who don't charter a vessel to go after fish, tackle cost is important.

The other day, I bought myself a complete new spinning rig. (The old reel was oxidized and the old rod was either rusted or eaten by locusts, I couldn't determine which.) Well, this little outfit set me back exactly eighty dollars and eighty-six cents. Why? Well, I'll tell you why.

I could have gotten a decent rig for about half that: rod, reel, monofilament line, doodads for lures—and possibly a can of varnish, free. But the tackle manufacturers have gotten mighty fancy, lately, and I am supposed to be an "authority" on angling—owing, as you've seen, to the amount of writing I've done, not the amount of fish catching. As an authority, I *have* to appear with the latest stuff, the gadgets and gimmicks. For if I walked up to a snook-hole, or waded out on a bonefish bank, with even the 1950 tackle, I'd *lose face. Prestige*. People would think I hardly knew a mullet from a scupper.

So I have to use this fancy gear. My present rod is made out of mica or maybe glass or possibly beryllium. My line is Dacron, Orlon, or maybe it's still nylon. I lose track. And the reel I bought is made, I believe, of an alloy that was released only last month by the Government as it had all been going, up to that time, into radar sets in the war heads of guided missiles. This kind of thing costs money and looks good. But not one damned fish has heard about any of it, so it doesn't matter to *them*. What I'm trying to say here is that, in my opinion, simple, straightforward tackle does the trick.

You look at a sports-goods catalogue. You will begin to feel that you are a piscatorial moron. Here you intended to go out with nothing more than two or three rods, some line, hooks and a bit of bait. Now you see you need shock-absorbers in your waders. Prevents stone bruises. You need a Geiger counter—might locate uranium on the trip. Your reels should be fashioned of Prysmex. Lightning resistant. You need balanced tackle, a matched set of rods, twelve in all, like golf clubs. I knew a man once, a multimillionaire in Palm Beach, who had sixteen graduated and balanced rods with his name and address shellacked on each one. "How," I asked him, "do you ever manage to get the right-sized fish to hit the suitable rod?"

This man soon gave up fishing.

I myself like to hang a fish on moderately light tackle for its size. Nevertheless, when I go trolling in the sea, I take along only two outfits. I take a heavy rod for big ones and a light rod with thirty-pound test line for everything else. In nearer shore, on the flats, I'm apt to take just my casting rod—the kind you use for bass—or even a trout rod. Some guides and many anglers maintain that thirty-pound test line is too small for sailfish, but I've never broken it even when taking big white marlin, and men have caught blue marlin of upward of three hundred pounds on such tackle.

When a salt-water game fisherman talks about tackle, though, he's talking in a different world from the fresh-water angler. You will get some idea of what I mean by that, in the pages ahead. It was revealed to me only slowly, over many years, and while other sportsmen were learning the same thing. Time was, when a really doughty man might cast salmon flies at baby tarpon. Nowadays, ocean anglers go after baby tarpon with trout rods and big tarpon with plug-casting outfits. The record is well over a hundred pounds in the latter sport.

My early days of sea fishing followed many years of trout, bass, pickerel, pike and muskie fishing. Naturally, when I saw myself taking fish routinely that weighed from twenty to eighty pounds, I thought the heavy gear then in use was essential. But I've since caught all of the same species on very light tackle and many of them on my old fresh-water rigs.

This brings me to another "confession."

It is obviously a lot of fun to roar out on the Atlantic, Pacific or Caribbean in a big motorboat, with a view to catching a fish of five hundred pounds or more. But it *is* expensive. And it is a lot of *work!* Your seafaring angler will enthrall a group of porch loafers with an account of the hours he battled a monster. I, too, many times, have battled for hours with monsters—losing most of them in the end, as admitted. But a day comes when many anglers of that type get old enough—or even wise enough—to desist.

For no matter how magnificent the thrill, no matter how Homeric the struggle, there is always a point in taking a very large fish when the angler realizes—realizes acutely—that he has set himself to do, *for fun*, something not unlike unloading a coal barge, alone, with a big shovel, fast—and no time off even for wiping sweat.

This awareness, which comes to all men, does not even correspond *precisely* to the basic concept implied by the word "fishing."

Some men, facing that somber truth, quit. Some others are told by their doctors that they must quit. Some, like me, don't exactly stop; but we cease to spend so much effort in the pursuit. Last time I went out when the tuna were running, for instance, I hung a whopper and after much toil fought him to the boat. He escaped when the mate reached for the leader. The next day, while Mrs. Wylie massaged liniment into my shoulders, I kept asking myself what in hell I had thought I was doing. If I'd never fought even one tuna, it might have been different. But there I'd been, pushing fifty, unloading that coal barge for the umpteenth time!

Before me, at the moment, is a letter which just arrived from one of the world's top anglers, Jack Mahony, of Miami. Jack has been president of the Rod and Reel Club of Miami Beach and a referee in the Cat Cay Tuna Tournaments. He wrote to discuss the matter of the seaways of tuna; but he mentioned in passing that he, too, was shunning the heavy fishes. Not because they'd worn him down but because he had always enjoyed a different kind of sea fishing even more. *Me, too!*

A man can fish in the sea almost exactly as he fishes in fresh water. The trout angler knows the intimate pleasure of wading streams and casting into pools. The bass fisherman drifts his happy days away, still-fishing; or perhaps he sends a singing plug under that old stump, into that little cove, alongside yonder rock. The plug caster has all the same fun as the golfer, and catches fish in the bargain. He fishes from a bank, a bridge, a skiff. But that kind of fun has not much attracted marine anglers, till lately.

When they looked at the sea, ocean anglers usually thought in terms of deep, far-out water. To be sure, a few of them, for years aplenty, have fished from beaches. California, the Carolinas, Montauk, are peopled every year with surf casters. But even they had special gear—gear contrived to make incredible casts out over the breakers, gear requiring a special skill of its own.

Hardly anybody stopped to think that wherever the sea

and the shore come together there are billions of coves, of land-locked ponds, of salt-water "creeks" and "rivers," fallen logs, rocks, weed patches and the like. Fewer still bothered to note that in many areas, such as around the Keys and the Bahamas, there are immense stretches of "flats," where a man in boots could wade as appropriately as in any trout stream. Indeed, during my first dozen or so Florida years, I never saw anyone but a surf caster or two in waders. Yet in these land-close, fishy-looking spots, fish live. Not pike, of course—but barracuda, which are like muskies; and not trout—but the snappers, which hit like bullets, and chiros, which are exactly like trout, except that they are bigger than most trout and they jump more, and more fantastically. These are samples. There are many other very spectacular game fishes besides. *Look:*

Barracuda, snapper (many kinds), chiro (as noted)

Pompano (delicious)

Sea trout (familiar)

Redfish (or channel bass, or drum)

Crevallé jacks (let black-bass fishermen try these!)

Horse-eye jacks (powerhouses)

Tarpon, tarpon and tarpon (!!!)

Blue runners (casuals)

Groupers (several sorts)

Bonefish (some say, the greatest of them all)

Permit (what old bonefishermen graduate to)

Jewfish (any size)

Ocean talley (rugged)

Queen triggers (ditto—and beautiful, too)

Margate (lunch)

Porkfish, angelfish, butterfly fish, rock beauties (all bottom-feeders, all to be caught still-fishing, all beautiful beyond dreaming)

Mackerel (you know)

Snook (a pikelike fighter)

Nearly all these fish hit top-water baits, or flies. I have taken nearly all, many times, from small boats, skiffs, rubber boats and from the bank; many by wading. They run from a pound or two up. And "up" means *up!* Several of these breeds (of which you may never even have heard) run from ten to thirty pounds and some, like tarpon, reach two hundred, while the jewfishes get to a half ton. Of course, we're talking about shallow water, where only "small" jewfish, for instance, might be found. "Small" still could mean *fifty pounds.*

Now, to an angler accustomed, when fishing, to catching a bass or two or perhaps a couple of pickerel, this lavish variety will come as the eighth wonder of the world. But my list is still only a *tiny sample.* There are, around the Keys, for instance, literally hundreds of species of fish, of which scores upon scores *might rise* to a fly cast into a quiet cove, *to a plug* dropped above a blue pothole. This I hold to be the *most* sensational sort of fishing.

It brings you scenery and scenic variety instead of the hot, steel-blue monotony of the open sea. It brings you every sort of challenge as to terrain, as to weed, log, coral, whatnot. And it brings you a shot at a near-infinite variety of fish of great weight and sportiness. From such fishing you seldom come home skunked. There's almost always something biting. And you frequently come in loaded down.

Furthermore, you can get a sample of it with a two-bit rod, a dollar reel and a ten-cent line!

That's the point I was driving at!

Here is everyman's marine angling. Here is a chance at such sport as old Ike Walton knew, times ten—and then squared.

In the Florida Keys, the Ten Thousand Islands, the Bay of Florida—there is fishing of this sort. It can be found in the Bahamas, the West Indies. I suspect that wherever the land meets any ocean, some fine top-water casting may be found. One never knows till one's tried.

That's the great thing about ocean fishing:

There are always *bigger* fish. Always *new* fish. Always new *ways* to fish. Always new *places*.

The unlikeliest things can happen.

Not many moons ago, up in Peconic Bay, I went fishing with a man and a small boy. Bottom-fishing, for porgies. Hardly, you will say, much of a sport for a man who holds a club record for white marlin, or for a v.-p. of the IGFA (which you will hear all about). Okay. We pulled up, started the motor, and went out for blues. Bluefish, that is. Bluefish fishing, as all Long Islanders know, is better than porgy fishing, sportswise.

The boy—let's call him Dan, since his name is Dan Lindner—had never caught anything as big as a bluefish. He was ten, then. Well, we didn't catch any bluefish either. It rained.

We got wet. Then the motor conked out—you know how it is —and we got wetter. It seemed the water bottle had been left ashore—and maybe you know how *that* is. We got thirsty. We'd already eaten the big bar of chocolate I had in my jacket. So we also hungered. We rowed—miles. And finally we started the motor and headed for home—keeping in near shore because we didn't want to row any more, if that —— motor failed again.

It wasn't bluefish water. It wasn't any kind of fishing water, so far as Dan's father or I knew. But I put a yellow feather over, anyhow, to troll, and I handed the rod to the boy.

Note the above. This is fishing wisdom. It represents Wylie at his best, as an angling authority. For there is one thing—and one thing *only*—I know for sure about angling: you have to do it in the water.

As long as there's water around, unless it's in a jug or a glass, you might as well offer a bait. There could be something —even something you never heard of, or saw.

Well, pretty soon Dan got a strike.

It wasn't any porgy—I could see that. It took line against his drag, a lot of line in haste. It darned near pulled him off the boat seat. And when he reeled, that fish fought. We stopped the motor. The fight became thoroughly classic, and thoroughly amazing—since we hadn't expected a strike at all. It couldn't be a bluefish, we argued, because the water was only about shoulder deep. So what *was* it?

Dan at last brought it to boat. There it was, a foot down, whizzing around, still full of war. I heaved it in. And it was not a fish I'd ever seen—alive. It was a striped bass. A striper. And a darned nice one, too! In those parts, a striped bass is tops amongst sports fish. So here sat a kid, ten years old, who'd taken his first striper, while the high executive of the International Game Fish Association (me) could only stare in awe, having never caught one! Until my dying day I shall not forget the joy, the pure elation, on young Dan's face.

Turned out—to my surprise—that toward the end of every summer a few stripers enter Peconic Bay and a few very lucky anglers catch some. Not trolling, though, as a rule. Very rarely have I had a bigger kick from fishing than that day. Vicarious? Well, I'm not so sure. . . .

It's nice to be able to take a powerboat to the Red Sea or to Tasmania and drag whole mackerel baits to find out what will "come up." But you can have darn near as much excitement, on a rainy afternoon, in many a local bay, with a boat rod and a yellow feather. If you have Dan Lindner along, you can, anyhow.

People tell you pretty odd things about sea fish. I hear, now and again, of sailfish in the Indian Ocean that weigh five hundred pounds, or are supposed to. Over in Bimini, the ichthyologists at the Lerner Lab are hooking something so big they cannot pull it up—hooking it half a mile deep, or more. Soldiers stationed in the Pacific islands tell me of two-hundred-pound wahoo out that-a-way. And my brother Max recounts throwing rocks at big octopi that walked on the beach—of Ceylon, I think it was. But all those matters—and a million more—will have to be looked into by other anglers.

Me—I'll settle for lesser game—for a striper magically caught on a rainy afternoon—for a medium tarpon, any day, on a plug. I haven't years enough, energy enough, money enough, to go on high adventures.

I merely have—high adventures where I am.

And write about them.

Indeed, I am a little ashamed to have complained at all in this preface—or so violently and publicly elsewhere, as you will learn from what follows—of my bad luck. For what I truly feel is this, that anyone who can fish at all is lucky to be doing it, irrespective of his catch. Besides that, I've had a kind of luck that many of my casting cronies envy loudly: I've earned more writing about fishing than ever I spent to do it. To them that seems unjust, a double-gain that should be outlawed by honest fates.

And so it is. It is more. For I also *enjoy the writing!*

It is my hope you will admire it.

This volume is my publisher's idea. Stan Rinehart is a fisherman—an angler of many degrees. He takes trout in Wyoming. He sits with me, bonefishing in Florida, where I live and where he has a home. He goes out in the Gulf Stream with me, sometimes, after big ones. "People," he recently said, "will like a collection of your fishing pieces. Reading about it is the next best thing to doing it."

Maybe so. Maybe so.

But, much as I like writing of it, much as you may want to read, I'm sure we'd *both* rather fish!

For I cannot say to you here:

"Turn to page so-and-so. Put on a Leaping Lena. Maybe one with yellow rings on it. Now. See that oölite outcrop? See the shadow of that submerged mangrove root? About in a line between them, I just saw something boil. Could have been a tarpon. Might have been a snook. Looked like a redfish to me. But whatever it is, it's big. Cast easy and let your plug float dead a second or two. Then give it a few little jumps. Then let it lie again. And be ready all the while for about half a stick of dynamite to let go under it!"

I can't say that, in a book.

You can't feel the wind, see the contours of the bottom as they are disclosed by the colors of the sea. You cannot hear the soft sounds we make in the boat, the jingle of hooks, the dribble of water from the oars; you can't smell the palmetto blossoms on the bank or hear the bees in them, or see the pileated woodpecker that had holed yonder dead palm trunk, or the roseate spoonbills flying against the azure sky. You can't spot that dark fin out on the shimmering water, can't squint and try to decide whether it's the caudal of a feeding permit or the dorsal of a shark, seen edge-on.

None of that—reading, writing.

Like me, you'd rather fish.

So this is just stopgap stall till vacation rolls around. Hope you go soon, then. And, *tight lines!* I won't wish you a full creel, though, because where the fishing in this book occurs, a creel wouldn't do. You might not be able to cram into a creel even the tail of the first one that hit.

Go see.

PHIL WYLIE

Some fish

That misunderstood fish—
the shark

Dread of sharks is a universal human fear. Landlubbers who have never seen the sea have a horror of it because the sea is full of sharks. Sailors, whose lives have been spent on salt water, are seldom cured of the sensation. On the contrary, they collect hundreds of shark legends from other maritime men and their fears are increased. No tale of a castaway or of a rueful party adrift in a lifeboat is complete without its "attack" by a shark or many sharks, its narrow escape, or its gruesome loss of a member to the ravening jaws of those formidable fishes.

3

Some fish

The average citizen, then, thinks a shark synonymous with death or at least, dismemberment. And there is nothing about the shark himself or his eerie cousins, the rays, to disappoint the observer. They are the most frightful-looking of all big creatures, with the exception of giant squids and octopi. The ghastly gape of a shark's jaw, the double semicircle of mighty teeth or sets of teeth, the malignant stare of fishy eye is awesome to behold. And any angler who has had a hooked fish assaulted by a shark knows the beast is capable of speed and fury; he knows also that the teeth and jaws are fully as destructive as they seem to be. A single bite of a big shark may take out of a tuna as much as a hundred pounds of meat!

The shark, moreover, like a death-dealing submarine and its raised periscope, often heralds his approach with the ominous cutwater of a dorsal fin. The sight of such a fin has frozen the hearts of men the world over, for thousands of years. On certain Australian beaches, lookouts are posted for sharks, and when one is sighted whistles summon all bathers from the water. During the Second World War, shark-repellent chemicals were issued to and worn by men liable to find themselves swimming. And all such facts make it appear that sharks are truly tigers of the sea, a horrid menace, greatly to be feared.

The trouble with such belief is that the more carefully it is checked the less absolute it proves to be. As a menace to man the shark, like the barracuda, has a reputation several thousand per cent bigger than his performance justifies. People have been bitten by 'cudas, beyond doubt, but not often. Live men have been destroyed by sharks. But how often?

In the forty-four years since it has kept official records of such events, the United States Navy has authentic accounts of at least two cases of sure shark bite, one followed by death, and a third "probable" case. There have been no fatal instances in the past eighteen years, according to these records, even though a great many thousand Americans spent untold man-hours in life jackets or merely swimming—in tropical, definitely shark-infested waters. The figures might be somewhat larger were it possible for every man seized by a shark to report the fact; some men so seized may have been presumed merely drowned. But the total would still be quite small! And too many thousands survived to leave room for the existing legends.

Technical Note Number 89 of the Navy's Bureau of Medicine and Surgery has this to say: "The shark is a wary fish, suspicious of noise, movement, and unfamiliar forms." In a booklet called *Shark Sense,* the Navy's Division of Aviation Training is more succinct: "There is very little danger from sharks." "People suffer more from shark fright than shark bite." "Don't believe anybody's shark stories, even if he can show you the ocean in which it happened." And it adds, for the benefit of men who actually find themselves in the sea, face to face with a shark, "If the truth were known, the shark probably is more frightened of you than you possibly can be of him."

A little reflection by the thoughtful reader will tend to indicate a basic validity in this official attitude. For, if sharks were as reckless and rampaging as they are imagined to be, deep-sea diving would be out of the question. No bubble-stream would scare the monsters. The diver's suit would be no

5

obstacle to teeth that can rend the toughest of all hides—the shark's own. Yet, somehow, divers don't seem to be devoured. Goggle-fishermen, furthermore, who wear no rubber suit and trail no bubbles, always come home for supper. Years pass without a report of shark bite from our summer seacoasts, though there are millions of bathers in the water—and millions of sharks. The classes in marine biology at the University of Miami, young ladies along with the young men, regularly descend in diving helmets to the coral reefs off Florida where lurk all manner and all sizes of sharks. Not even one lush co-ed has been lost.

This author has, on occasion though not by design, swum cheek by jowl with various sharks of various weights and, to date, has suffered greater injury from mosquitoes. Yet I know, of what lawyers call "my own knowledge," which means directly, of three people who have been bitten by sharks. None was killed. One had to have an arm amputated. The other two recovered without permanent injury. In every instance, however, the sharks involved were of the so-called harmless variety and of small size—not "man-eaters" but fifty or sixty-pounders. And in every case, the man bitten had first shoved, socked, swatted, stuck or tried to harpoon the shark! A little shark, a black-tip or a nurse shark, assaulted by a human being, can and sometimes does turn around and bite his assailant. A mouse does the same thing, exactly.

It would be useful, indeed, to be able to say what sharks would bite what people under what conditions. For small sharks, the answer seems to be, if you start the argument. For the monsters, however, perhaps the real "reason" for the attack

6

on a live human being may never be entirely clear. It may be, simply, an individual matter. Biologists used to think animals of each species followed rigid behavior patterns; only in recent years have they come to know that even amongst such lowly life forms as insects, behavior varies enormously from bug to bug. Here and there among mankind are to be found homicidal maniacs; here and there among the great white sharks, the tiger sharks, and others, may be a "homophagic" individual, a brute with a taste for you and me.

The unusual rapacity of the sharks off Australia is probably owing to the abundance of sharks and the comparative scarcity of food. One doubts that Australians taste better than other people. It is even barely possible that some Australian sharks have "learned," locally, a bit about the edibility and defenselessness of a swimming person. And there is cause to suspect that an individual shark, having once dined on a human corpse (and sharks are scavengers), may try a livelier sample.

A series of shark attacks along the New Jersey and New England coasts some years ago was thought to be the work of a single animal. A corpse, since it does not move or make a noise and since, in time, it exudes the evidence of its decayed condition, is natural prey for a shark. Men, having assumed from time immemorial that they are the favored meal, open the bellies of such sharks as they catch. When they find human bones therein, their horrors are "confirmed" and they do not even wonder whether the human being was taken alive or not. From that day on, they "know" sharks are man-eaters; the slender fact is padded with what is, nearly always, myth.

From the point of view of statistical danger it's undoubtedly far safer to swim in "shark-infested" waters than, say, to go on playing golf in a thundershower. A man who fell overboard amongst a pack of madly feeding sharks might easily be out of luck. It is hazardous to attack sharks when in the water with them—even very small sharks. The Navy, taking no chances, still puts nets out when swimming parties are held alongside a ship. So the fundamental rule, I think, is to avoid sharks if you can; but, if you encounter them while swimming, to remain calm. For, as the Navy booklet suggests, more people have doubtless suffered a greater aggregate of heart and nerve damage from fear of sharks than the total loss of man-years in shark dinners. A corollary might be added: The "shark-repellents" used during the last war do not appear to be especially effective; what keeps the sharks away seems to be not the chemical but the innate dread sharks have of live people.

To the average person, then, the question concerning sharks is the one of people-eating. That morbid an 1 vastly exaggerated concern is most unfortunate because sharks and their relatives are amongst the most fascinating of living things. They are "living fossils," to begin with. They appeared some three hundred and fifty million years ago and are not much changed in that long reach of time although, before there were men on the earth, sharks were bigger—sometimes a hundred and fifty feet long! Sharks are amongst the toughest and most viable of living things. As a marine "crop" they have countless uses—and could have more than they do. They are good to eat. And at least one member of the vast family—the sting ray, of all things—makes an interesting pet! Because of

8

fear and loathing, we have neglected sharks. Suppose, because bulls gore people, we had done without beef, milk, cowhide, cheese and ice cream?

It often seems to me that the attitude toward sharks is a good example of the way people form all sorts of *prejudices*. Sharks look different from other fish and are sometimes dangerous. Gradually, perhaps because sharks can be identified by people who cannot tell apart any other breed of fishes, sharks have been given the blame for all the fish-biting in the seven seas. It's not fair! During the war, bathing was prohibited for our troops stationed on Asuncion Island; two men had been eaten alive by a school of trigger fish—little fellows of a pound or two apiece. The bite of the coral-reef eel, the moray, is well known amongst anglers. Men working on marine construction in tropical waters—and divers—fear the blind, bone-cracking lunge of the jewfish. The barracuda and the fresh-water pirahna can bite. Fishermen know that almost any caught, toothed specimen, if it gets a chance, will sink its teeth in human tissue; that goes for a pike or a snapper or a wahoo —one of which last species took a large chunk out of the fore-arm of a charterboatman known to me. But, though sharks don't bite nearly as often or as readily as is assumed, and though other fishes bite oftener and with less provocation, sharks get the worst reputation which, as I say, is the way all prejudices are formed.

Sharks are not only personally tough and rugged but they are durable from the evolutionary point of view. They were around back in the dinosaur days and probably earlier—and are here still, though the dinosaurs long since gave way to pos-

9

sibly rougher species, such as men. Some sharks lay eggs; others produce live young; in either case, the instant a new shark emerges in its watery world it is all set with the suitable instincts and bodily tools to hunt, fight, eat and generally survive.

The shark might be said, in fact, to be Nature's most "all-out" experiment with *teeth*. A shark is a biological engine behind teeth. Many sorts, perhaps most, have several rows of teeth in their mouths. The front row is vertical, the rearward rows slant toward the gullet. Let a front tooth be lost and a tooth behind moves up to take its place. Shark teeth are set in cartilage and the loss of one incurs no bleeding, perhaps no pain. The whole creature, furthermore, is boneless in the technical sense of bone. His bonelike tissue is really cartilage—and a shark can survive more terrible injury than nearly any other living thing. He can, that is, take it as well as dish it out.

Sharks, as a rule, are also covered from snout to tail with what are called "denticles" and amount to small teeth. Such minutely toothed skin is known as shagreen; and shark leather is the toughest in the world.

Sharks, furthermore, have adapted themselves to all sorts of conditions—varying water temperature, countless sorts of food and, as few people know, even to *fresh* water. There is a body of fresh water known as Lake Nicaragua which contains not only sharks but skates and rays. The lake was once probably a part of the sea; volcanic action closed it off; tributaries gradually diluted its salt content until today it is entirely fresh. But the dilution was slow and the shark population had time

10

to adjust. It did. So it's hard to kill a shark even by geological means!

How hard it is to kill one by hand and in person is testified by Captain Art Wills of the *Sea Queen*—a charterboat berthed at Miami Beach. On a Bimini fishing expedition, the *Sea Queen* "raised" a mako shark. The big fish gave the angler the fight of his life but, after something over two hours, was brought to gaff.

"We got a tail rope on the mako," Captain Wills once told me, "and heaved him aboard. He was a big one, well over four hundred. Still full of fight. I clubbed him with a heavy billy —often and hard enough to kill a dozen blue marlin. He still had a wiggle left. So I broke out an ice pick and stabbed him, by actual count, twenty-three times, in what I thought was the brain at every clip—and what I was sure would be the brain, in twenty-three tries. Then I lashed him with new rope across the stern. His head hung overboard on one side of the boat, his tail on the other. We started in. And all of a sudden I saw that mako begin to tense himself against the rope."

Captain Wills is a sanguine man, as a rule. I've seen him merely chuckle when two hundred and fifty pounds of blue marlin (on my line) charged into the stern of the *Sea Queen* and drove his bill deep in the mahogany. At this moment, however, Art Wills admits he was excited:

"One of the rope strands snapped! I couldn't believe it! Luckily the mako had swallowed the bait and we'd left the hook, leader and line where it was. Nobody in his right mind would reach into even a presumably dead mako's mouth to

11

get back a hook! I yelled at the passenger who'd caught the mako to grab his rod and get back in the fighting chair—just in case. Good thing. The 'in case' was fact, seconds later. That beat-up, stabbed, 'dead' mako gave one enormous heave, snapped all the line around it and went overboard." Captain Wills paused here and shook his head as if he hardly believed it himself. "We had to fish the fish all over again. It took another *hour* before the angler could bring him to gaff a second time. When he did, we made doggone sure we wouldn't lose him overboard again. We lashed him under the canopy and we not only disconnected his brain from the rest of him with a knife, but we sat on him all the way in!"

That's a pretty high score in viability—the sheer power to stay alive.

Until quite recently, nobody understood how to do a good tanning job on a shark's hide. But in 1920, a Dane in Copenhagen named Brodo Bendixen discovered a method. Later that same year an American, Theodore H. Kohler, found a chemical solution that would dissolve the flinty denticles without ruining the leather underneath. Properly tanned, shagreen is very beautiful; it is flexible and resists wear and scuffing as does no other animal material. As far as I can find out, no great amount of shark leather is in common use—though it ought to be. Perhaps it is a matter of public education. Certainly anybody who has raised a child wouldn't mind a good-looking, much tougher leather than any present sort for those schoolday shoes!

The "wily" Orientals, who have been ahead of us "civilized" Westerners in so many things, knew about shark leather long ago. They used it, denticles and all, to cover the grip of sword handles. It was a very practical idea since handles so covered never got slippery—no matter how much blood was spilled on them.

Shark meat is, of course, edible. Probably millions, even tens of millions of Americans have eaten the meat of sharks or related fish without knowing it. "Grayfish," for example, is a commercial term for such meat—usually the meat of the small dog shark. In times when scallops were scarce and the price high, commercial fishermen have been known to bang out little cylinders of meat from the flippers or "wings" of rays and skates with a gadget like a cooky cutter. This meat, crumb-dipped, fried in deep fat, covered with tartar sauce, is eaten for scallop by myriads who can't tell the difference. And of course, the Chinese consider shark-fin soup amongst the world's major table delicacies. In taste, the meat of a mako shark is said to be a dead ringer for swordfish—high praise, indeed. And the fairly recent discovery that shark liver is rich in vitamins has led to a whole new fishing industry. A shark's liver, incidentally, is about a quarter of the beast, by weight—so the vitamin hunters get an excellent return on every specimen they take.

An informal, lunch "club" of anglers to which I belong (in the sense that any fisherman who drops by is a "member" for that day) was used some years ago as a test group in the matter of shark edibility. Somebody in the crowd had caught a small hammerhead. The baleful-looking critter was carefully butchered, filleted, and served one noon for everybody's lunch. When the members had finished the meal, all expressed themselves as pleased with the anonymous fish course and one even went so far as to say it was the "best damn fish" he'd ever eaten in that particular restaurant—which may or may not have been the highest possible praise for the meat of hammerhead sharks. The "members" were then told what they'd eaten and, being fishermen, weren't distressed. They'd enjoyed their lunch; but the prejudice still holds even among such salty people: no one ever brought in and ordered up hammerhead fillets again.

The habits and seaways of sharks are still mysterious. Vast, technical volumes have been published on the subject by brilliant ichthyologists, yet whole departments of shark conduct still remain unknown. The same region of the sea will sometimes abound in sharks and at others, under what appear to be identical conditions, sharks will be harder to find there than pileated woodpeckers in big timber. Nobody knows why. That fact, during the last war, once occasioned me intense embarrassment.

People who write a great deal about fish and fishing are logically presumed to know whereof they speak. Wherefore, early in the war, along with Michael Lerner of the International Game Fish Association, Erl Roman, the noted angler and present sole instructor in angling in a university, various officers and enlisted men, OSS personnel, boats, a blimp and tons of gear, I joined an expedition designed to study the best means of survival for men cast adrift from sunken boats and for plane crews in the same predicament.

One of our projects was to demonstrate for photographic illustration how, if sharks began to swarm around your life-

14

boat, life raft or rubber boat, you could drive them off by banging them in the snout with oars. We figured that all we had to do to get suitable pictures for the proposed training manual was to go where sharks were thick, chum them up with chopped fish, row out in various types of life craft, bait a few sharks in close—and smite them, before the cameras. So we fared forth in Coast Guard vessels to a site on the reefs off the Florida Keys where, ordinarily, it was difficult to catch a fish on hook and line owing to the prevalence of hungry sharks which would swipe your fish before you could reel it in.

To make absolutely certain that our life rafts and rubber boats would be pictured amidst veritable swarms of big sharks, we took along twelve milk cans full of steer blood—brought to the Keys by jeep from Miami's slaughterhouses.

We anchored in a spot selected by myself, by Buddy Carey —then in service and now a fine charterboatman—and by the late Bill Hatch, a world-famed fishing guide, as ideal "shark grounds." We began to pour chum into the current along the edge of the Gulf Stream. In addition, we slowly poured the blood. Messrs. Lerner, Roman, Wylie and Carey rowed out into this baited region in a variety of vessels. I cannot speak for the others, but my own state of mind was faintly apprehensive, to understate it. A rubber boat makes you feel that between you and the sea and its steam-shovel-jawed inhabitants is a bit of fabric no thicker than one side of a hot-water bottle. And a meat-filled, gory sea is supposed to drive sharks crazy.

We waited. The crimson slick stretched out behind the Coast Guard vessel—for yards, rods, half a mile, a visible red

15

mile. But no sharks appeared. Hours went by. Down below were the coral caverns and pinnacles where sharks had always been. Out at sea was the purple Gulf Stream which is known to be shark-infested. But nary a shark did we lure that day by our overwhelming methods. Why? Too much blood? I doubt it. Some "condition"—such as a prior abundance of food—which made them refuse to "show"? I doubt that, also. They just weren't around that day, in my opinion. They were elsewhere. They were having a shark convention in some other part of the ocean. It was their day off. It was something, anyhow, which the ichthyologists and the old-timers couldn't explain—but it happened.

Nobody knows completely and for sure, even within a single breed of some sharks, where they go or when or why. Makos, for example, are presumed to be migrants that travel enormous ranges, alone, perhaps at times in groups. But I have a keenly observant friend named Ralph Ruhl who is, professionally, a nurseryman, horticulturist, hibiscus-hybridizer and landscape architect. By temperament, he is a naturalist; by hobby, an angler. Several times, over a period of years, he has seen what he swears to be the same mako shark in the same spot and he has somewhat proven that claim by twice hooking (and twice losing) that "same" mako, from a small boat. So it is with considerable confidence that I state a theory of my own: When everything is known about sharks, what we know now will seem like a few drops in a very big bucket.

One kind of knowledge we have in fair abundance—knowledge about sharks as game fish. Some are; some aren't. In the earlier days of fishing, sportsmen tangled with sharks

16

(and all sorts of other "monsters" and "devils" of the deep, from mantas to spiny lobsters) with whatever gear they considered appropriate. Lances, harpoons, steel cable, rifles and elephant guns, super-gaffs, harpoon guns and the like were commonly used. If a man could have mounted a cannon on his boat, he would have employed that. In his book *Battles with Monsters of the Sea*, a doughty Englishman named F. A. Mitchell-Hedges describes graphically any number of such lurid encounters.

As time has passed, however, and as sports fishing has grown up, more and more men have begun to catch bigger and bigger sharks on standard marlin tackle and the like. A rod, that is, a big reel, a fairly heavy line and plenty of it, a large hook, a metal leader and a whole fish for bait. It was found that, under such conditions, the sharks which most closely resembled other game fishes in fighting tactics were the mackerel sharks—the mako and the porbeagle, also the white, the black-tip and perhaps the thresher. The mako, when hooked, is a leaping fish and some claim it can outjump any other fish in the sea. A small black-tip shark—say a thirty-pounder—hooked on a plug and fought on black-bass tackle, will give any expert a handful of lunging, leaping, surging trouble. I have seen a white shark of enormous size "greyhound"—leap in long drives, that is—twenty feet at a time and over and over, as if some more formidable sea monster were pursuing it. But I've never hooked one.

Erl Roman, the angling "professor" and author mentioned above, reports he once fought a three-hundred-pound white shark for more than three hours on twenty-four-thread line with a stout rod and a 10/0 reel and broke it off when the shark showed no signs whatever of tiring. The rest of the party on board began to grow weary of standing by doing nothing! "To catch that shark," Earl said, "might have cost them all a whole day's fishing. I didn't want it that badly so I broke the line." Now there, I submit, is a real sportsman!

In the opinion of the late Zane Grey, an angler with a world of almost world-wide experience (and also, I believe, in the opinion of my friend Ernest Hemingway, who is a rare fisherman), the mako is the top game fish. A mako shark is not a tawny, gray, gray-brown or greenish-brown shark; its back and sides are blue and its belly is white. Its nose is sharply pointed, its teeth are horrendous. And from the description given here of its "viability," the stamina of the mako as a fighting fish can be estimated. Many an angler with marlin and tuna experience behind him has been forced, at long, reluctant last, to give up on a mako.

In Bimini waters (off the British Bahamas) mako sharks commonly attack hooked, giant bluefin tunas. Along with multitudes of anglers I've brought whopping tunas close to the boat—within a minute or two of gaffing—only to have the cobalt torpedo of a mako sluice into view, bite a huge hole in my tunas and so disqualify them as a "fair caught" fish. And many an old-timer, upon discovering a mako in the vicinity of his hooked tuna, has abandoned the tuna in an attempt to catch the shark.

In the spring, tunas cruise past Bimini in huge schools; they look like fleets of baby submarines; how many millions go by each year, nobody knows. But they are plentiful in their season and mako sharks are always rare. So numerous anglers will gladly give up a tuna for a shot at a mako. How scarce makos are may be gathered from the fact that in all my twenty-odd years as a deep-sea angler, in all the hundreds and hundreds of days I've trolled in mako ranges, I've never caught one and was never certain that I'd even hooked one.

The thresher shark is even rarer in those ranges. So far as I know, only one has ever been taken on rod and reel near Bimini.

Thresher sharks have an upper caudal fin, or tail fin, about as long as their bodies. This fin is strong, flexible and equipped with an oval enlargement at the tip, so it somewhat resembles a limber club. The thresher uses its tail to kill fish, swimming into a school and flailing furiously—from which habit comes its name. The fish in question, brought in at Cat Cay, had struck a trolled bait *with its knobbed tail!* The hook had been imbedded in the tail; and the thresher was fought backwards as a result—the "hard way."

There is one report, by a credible angler, of the hooking of a thresher shark from shore. The angler was casting out from a tiny rock emergence in the sea—hardly big enough to be called an island. He states that the thresher he hooked swam in close to the rock and tried, by wild swings of its tail, to knock him and his rod and reel off the rock and into the water where, presumably, the thresher planned to deal with its dilemma under conditions more favorable to sharks than anglers.

Any shark, if he is big enough, will give the rod-and-reel angler a workout. The hammerhead, common off Miami and greatly though unduly feared, probably owing to the frightful

Some fish

look of his eye-stalks and the protruding eyes at their ends, is neither especially fast nor particularly aggressive. Nevertheless, if a big one takes a bait, the angler is in for some fast runs, some hard lunges and a long, dogged scrap. In taking out a novice who would like, eventually, to get a marlin, I often try to spot the fin of a basking hammerhead. A couple of hours with one, on marlin gear, is excellent practice.

The sum of all we know about sharks suggests most of all that we have much more to learn. They can and do bite and even devour human beings under conditions that are never quite predictable. Yet the fear of sharks is disproportionate. A statistical examination of the millions of us who swim in the sea and the millions who walk on city streets makes it quite evident that, if we were *logical*, we'd be several hundred times as afraid of automobiles as of sharks.

In all the great groups of fishes, sharks, among the oldest, are among the most varied and interesting. The sea is full of them—as the plains were once populous with buffalo; sharks would be far harder to exterminate; and we have only begun to find their uses as drug sources, as food, as leather, as fertilizer. Many more uses will be exploited in the great ranges of the sea; some day, no doubt, shark ranching will be a solid business enterprise.

We who go down to the sea in ships (and rowboats) to fish know that many a kind of shark is a gamester worthy of the most skillful angler's mettle—and that goes for little blacktips on fly rods as much as for the great mako, on marlin tackle. But our human aversion to the breed has prevented us from getting as well acquainted with sharks as we might. And, with acquaintance, our feelings could change.

There used to be, in Key West, an impounded arm of the sea, a salt pond, fixed up as an aquarium by the proprietors of a restaurant and night club. Here many ocean fish were kept alive and fed by hand for the entertainment of customers. Among them was a shark—a little one of perhaps forty pounds. The son of the proprietor had grown fond of the shark and, after feeding it for many weeks, had discovered the beast liked to be scratched. It would swim up to shore when the ground was rhythmically stamped. It would then lift its head out of water and rest it on a stone. The young boy would feed it and scratch it as if it were a kitten. In due course, the boy discovered the shark had such confidence in him that he could seize it bodily, drag it out of water, hold it in his arms, or scratch it while it lay on the ground. By and by, of course, the shark would want to return to the water—but only after several minutes of being a "pet shark."

At the Lerner Marine Laboratories, in Bimini, it was found not long ago that stingarees, the touchy and terrible cousins of sharks, responded in a similar way to similar treatment. Here, for the purposes of scientific research and observation, hundreds of large ocean fish are maintained alive in big "pens" built in the pellucid harbor. Sting rays, which live well and take food readily under such conditions, would, ordinarily, if you touched them, drive the barbed, needle-sharp, six-inch "stinger" clean through your arm—and leave it there as a dangerous and agonizing surgical problem. But, nowadays, when feeding time comes at the laboratory stockades, the sting-arees—monsters as broad as an oriental rug—swim placidly up to the vertical wall where the man with their bucket of small fish stands and flap themselves two-thirds of the way out of water to be fed directly by hand—and to have their backs scratched!

So it may be that our shark-approach had been wrong for milleniums. Sharks are mechanized sets of teeth, sure. They can bite, beyond doubt. But when dealt with in a friendly fashion (rather than by cannon and harpoon), they seem willing to be pals. I'm not ready to try palling up with a loose, "wild" shark —but on the other hand, I've reached the stage I recommend to you: the word "shark" doesn't paralyze me and the sight of a periscopelike dorsal fin, gliding around where I am swimming, doesn't fill me with the sensation my last hour has come. Also, I don't kill all sharks on sight for no reason, as many deep-sea anglers do. Living sharks have let me live, time and again; but like the sharks themselves, I'm a shade wary of the other guy; I can't quite lose that "What-big-teeth-you-have-grandma" feeling, even though I've gradually found sharks to be a lot more interesting than horrifying. I'm sure, if I ever have a salt-water pond of my own, there'll be a pet shark in it. Not a very big one, though.

There are no average *sailfish*

Nobody knows what is in the mind of a fish—or whether he has one. Some people merely know more than others about how fishes behave. And, from the behavior, they invent fishly states of mind. The moods and humors of brook trout, for example, have absorbed the time and discernment of millions of men for generations—men in the barefoot-boy stage, the investigating-scientist stage and the retired-millionaire stage. Books have been written about why trout do what they do and what trout, supposedly, feel. But there is not much of this sort of information on the sailfish, and there should be.

Some fish

In the era before the sailfish was commonly taken on rod and reel, marine angling was regarded by fresh-water sportsmen as decidedly second-rate—not an art, just a branch of commercial fishing. The tarpon, it is true, was an early exception but, somehow, the mere fact that this fish, when so moved, will enter fresh water and even live in lakes, qualified him as semimarine. People went kingfishing; people caught jewfish in the sea, on ropes; people hand-lined for bottom fish. And then they found out how to catch sailfish. It was the beginning of a new age for the angler.

Well do I remember my first one. I was trolling straight back from the stern of a Miami charterboat—the line, twenty-four-thread; the reel, a 6/o on a pretty heavy rod. My bait was an eight-inch strip of belly cut from one of the bonitas we had been catching. I could see it plainly, flickering and skipping in the clean, choppy water some thirty feet astern.

"Here comes a sail!" the skipper yelled.

I didn't see anything, I was watching the bait.

"Underneath it . . . behind it!" The skipper tried to tell me where to look, but I was too excited and too much of a neophyte to see the surging mass of chocolate brown that is a submerged sail on a sunny day. I did see his bill. It came out of water at an angle and looked like a black stick. I felt a minnowlike tap. And that was all.

"Drop back!" the captain shouted.

For a moment, I couldn't think what he meant. I forgot that a sailfish usually swats his quarry with his "sword" —which is more like a long, rattail file—and then lets it settle in the sea, stunned, before he gobbles it up. This particular sailfish, however, was hungry enough to try again, even though (and it must have surprised him) his first crack at my bait didn't "kill" it. He put up his great purple dorsal, surfaced and rushed—again swatting the strip of belly, harder this time. This time I dropped back—that is, I threw the reel on free spool and allowed the line to run out, thumbing the spinning spool enough so it wouldn't backlash.

The result of that, naturally, was to stop the bait dead in the sea. In those days, we counted to ten—slowly—before striking. Most people still do. And all persons who have had the experience will certify that those ten seconds are emotionally wearing.

The bait sinks out of sight. The sailfish disappears in its general vicinity. The boat goes away from the scene at its steady four or five or six knots. Meanwhile the angler gets set to drive home the hook, knowing now that he has had a sailfish rise and a strike, but not at all certain that the fish will devour what it has swatted. At the end of ten seconds the angler throws on the drag again, lets the line tighten and, the instant he feels the weight of his fish, strikes back against it swiftly and strongly, three or four times. I did these things that day.

With the third backward drive of the rod, the sailfish put on his second personal appearance. Something in the strip bait he had just taken into his mouth was annoying him, pulling him around, sticking into him. The thing to do was to shake it out, pronto. So, in two or three seconds after my first heave, he drove straight up into the air—all seven feet and fifty pounds of

25

him—his sail spread full, his bills open wide and his great blue eyes rolling with—what? Fear and horror? Hate and fury? Something.

He leaped high enough to walk under if there had been a walk, hit with a mighty splash, leaped again and repeated, four or five times. Everybody on board was yelling. They told me, "You hung him, boy!" They advised me to, "Look at that baby jump!" I knew I had hung him and I could see him jump.

I could also feel him. Indeed, he was loosening up my shoulder joints preparatory to yanking off my arms. However, the rod butt was firmly seated in a gimbal—a sort of universal joint below the front edge of my chair seat, and I am a fairly strong citizen, and very determined. The sailfish undertook, in the ensuing dozen seconds, the two-hundred-yard dash, submerged. I had, before that time, caught trout, bass, pickerel, pike, muskies and some smaller sea fish. This was my first experience in hooking the equivalent of a naval torpedo driving for an enemy warship.

At the end of the dash, the sailfish paused and tried leaping again. Then, begrudging every inch, he permitted me to horse, or pump, or heave him back toward the boat about three quarters of the distance. At that point it occurred to him that perhaps he could rid himself of the oral nuisance by sounding, and down he went, a hundred feet or so. I horsed him back, inchmeal. He leaped again—took to greyhounding and tail-walking—tried to circumnavigate the boat, and ran out of ideas until I had him alongside. Then, just as the skipper seized the leader and reached over to grab his bill in a gloved hand, he jumped one more mean time.

After that, the skipper got him. He heaved the flopping monster up along the ship's side, and the mate dispatched him with a truncated version of a police billy. Tenderly, then, he was brought aboard. He seemed to come to, eyed us dolefully, and whacked the deck with his tail. My friends admired him and eagerly inspected his incredible colors until they faded. Me, I was too beat-up, shaky and generally dazed to see much of that.

I have been at some pains to describe this event for the reason that it records the perfectly typical taking of a perfectly typical sailfish. Twenty-eight minutes had elapsed from the moment the fish struck to the moment the skipper dispatched the fish. A little longer than seven feet, a little more than fifty pounds in weight, the fish was about average. And, in the average taking of the average sail, there is only one major difference today, and one minor.

The major difference lies in the now-common use of outriggers for sailfishing, two of which are usually carried by the deep-sea fishing cruiser. An outrigger is equipped with a halyard like that used for raising a flag. The halyard is provided with an ordinary snap clothespin. In this, a twist of the angler's line is pinched, and the clothespin is run to the tip of the outrigger, so that the line extends from rod, aloft to clothespin and thence back down to the sea.

The outrigger trolls the bait outside the ship's wake, which is regarded as an advantage, and, since it holds the bait from so high a point, often yanks it clear out of water as the boat rocks or pitches, giving the bait all the action of a flying fish. When a sailfish hits such a bait, the line is pulled out of the clothespin, a large amount of slack falls onto the sea, and thus the bait automatically and instantly "dies" in the water until the forward run of the boat takes up that slack. The angler using an outrigger doesn't have to remember to "drop back"—freespool his reel after the strike.

That makes sailfishing easier. And the minor change is the increasing popularity of light tackle for sailfish.

Now, as I've shown, there is a typical behavior for the strike and the fight of a sailfish. But there must be a qualification made concerning that statement: precious few sailfish seem to know what is expected of them—and it is this fact which gives character to the species and variety to the sport of taking it. Too damned much variety, as a rule.

For example, I once had a friend who was an old salmon angler and who held deep-sea fishing in low opinion. Thinking to change his mind, I took him out for sails. We will call this person Mr. Jerkins, because he turned out to be a bit of a jerk. It was the middle of winter—January—and, naturally, I explained that sailfish were scarcest in the winter and we'd be lucky even to see one. So, of course, we saw about fifty that day.

I got Mr. Jerkins set in the stern of the boat, myself alongside with a light rod and line, and I told him to relax, as we would doubtless be trolling for hours without action of any sort. Two minutes later, a double-header rose behind our two baits. Naturally, I instructed Mr. J.—for the tenth time—in dropping back.

These two sails, however, were born crazy. Or stupid. They had no plan to swat our baits and then wait for them to sink. They rose, fanned the air with their purple fins and

28

rushed. When they hit, they simply gulped both baits. I was an old fisherman, by then, and so I struck forthwith and hooked my fish. Jerkins, however, dropped back and his sailfish, feeling a hook in his mouth and having the convenience of a slack line—supplied because of my instructions—jumped lightly once into the air and threw the hook.

Mr. J. saw what happened and told me he ought to have hit it instanter, like any salmon. Reluctantly, I had to agree. My fish, meanwhile, was sizzling between sea and sky and he was watching it with interest. I handed the rod to him. "Take him in—get the feel of the power in him—get some practice."

Mr. J. took the rod. The instant he did, that particular sailfish acted as if it had been chloroformed. He sulked a little, waggled his fins feebly and allowed himself to be boated with no further fight. I have seen sailfish give up because they have been hooked deep in their interiors, or in the eye. This fish was hooked in the jaw, where he felt nothing except restraint. But he quit.

When he was boated, Mr. Jerkins said softly, "So that's the battling sailfish, eh?"

We baited up again and I began to pray quietly for another opportunity. One came along, presently. It rose up to within a dozen feet of the surface under my bait. As I was anxious to get Mr. J. hitched to an infuriated sail, I reeled in cautiously and lifted my bait out. The sail, a brown blur down below, moved over to the other bait, rose, and hit like a thunderclap. Mr. Jerkins dropped back—we waited without breathing—and he struck. Instantly the sail came raging out of the sea.

Some fish

I began to relax as I saw my companion tense and look worried. But, again, after that second jump, the fish seemed to lose interest. Once more Jerkins hauled it in without much struggle. When it came alongside, I peered over and saw that, in the first twisting leap, the fish had thrown a half hitch of the leader wire around its tail. This had come tight with the result that the sail was bent like a bow—the leader the bowstring—and it couldn't swim at all. I explained this, but Mr. J. seemed skeptical.

Mr. J. got his last hit just before he went in. A beautiful afternoon—a calm, sapphire sea and the sun getting ready to paint pictures on the western cloudscape. Only, when he hung the sailfish, being lucky, or maybe even a good angler for all I'll ever know, he also hung about three bushels of sargasso weed. This golden, tangled stuff fouled his leader, suffused itself over the face, fins and person of the fighting fish, and slowed him down to zero. Again, with no difficulty, Mr. Jerkins heaved in fish and encumbering mass of weed.

"So that's sailfishing," he repeated as we went in. "Hunh!"

He won't go out again—goes to Maine for salmon—and he tells all comers that sea fishing is just an old man's pastime.

An old man's pastime. The phrase haunts me.

I think of another friend of mine—a man named George —who was cruising toward the keys, towing a dinghy, when he noticed that there were two sailfish jumping around sportively on the near sea. An idea struck him. He baited up for sail, cut his motors, stepped aboard the dinghy and began to troll from there. Sure enough, one of the sailfish rose and hit. George dropped back and struck and hung the fish. His companions then cut loose the dinghy, which was what George had planned.

There he was, at sea in a rowboat, with a large sailfish on his line. The fish did some expert leaping at first, and every time it surged into the air, the dinghy rocked and shipped water. George was on his knees on a middle seat at the time.

"The last jump of the first series," George recounted, "threw me flat on my pan. When I got up, I had a bloody nose and the sail was running. The skiff picked up speed and for the next quarter hour we went for a sleigh ride around the ocean. Then the son of a gun quieted down and I began getting in line.

"I couldn't be sure whether I was pulling him to me, or the skiff to him, but, anyhow, we came together. Close. At this point it occurred to me I was without gloves, and without a billy to hit him with. How was I going to boat him? While figuring on that, I see that he is figuring, too. I swear he was lying there looking straight at me—his eye as big as a teacup and ornery as a wild pig's—figuring. Pretty soon he jumped, not merely out, but at me.

"He jumped on this side of the skiff and on that side. He'd pull against me and then spring out and the line would go slack and I'd flounder over backward. Don't know how many times he threw me. Maybe six. Anyhow, he stayed within twenty feet of me and I finally realized he was thinking of getting in there with me and sparring it out.

"At least, I began to see that one of those jumps—accidentally or on purpose—might make us shipmates. I thought, too, maybe he'd ram. I've heard of marlin trying that—on

31

purpose or in a blind rage—and I began to wish I hadn't bothered with this notion of dinghy-fishing for sail.

"Then what? He took a long, hard, mean run straight to the cruiser and my damned fool mate tried to gaff him as he went past. Don't never gaff a sail if you can help it. It just makes 'em twenty times as devilish.

"The gaff caught him in the shoulder. The mate heaved, the fish came out of water and raked a long mark on my cruiser with his bill. Then he broke the line, shook himself off the gaff, and me—I fell back again and this time, overboard. Never have I gone after a sail in a dinghy since."

The advice about not gaffing sailfish is sound. And the need of a stout pair of gloves for grabbing one by the bill—the conventional method of taking a sailfish—was brought home to me long ago. My friend, Larry Schwab, the writer and theatrical producer, had a handsome cruiser named the *Pirate Wench* on which he was wont to cruise amongst the keys and islands. A good mariner but not an expert angler then, he had sometimes fished from his yacht but never had taken a sail from her.

By that time, I'd caught a dozen or more and felt thoroughly able to act as a guide. I said that I would go out with him and get him a sailfish. His captain would run the boat—he and Mildred, his wife, would fish—and I'd be the mate. It worked, somewhat to my astonishment. We went out to the edge of the Gulf Stream. We baited up. Larry and Mildred began to troll, straight back. Pretty soon a fish rose behind Mildred's bait and, with none of the aplomb common to fishing guides, I told her what to do. She did it. Pretty soon she was fighting one lively sail.

Remember now, that I was responsible for boating that fish. The captain had had no experience in such matters. While Mildred fought the sailfish—and it battled her as if its life were in danger, which it was (the sea was rough, too, which added to the battle an element of lift, rock, yaw and nose dive) —as she fought, I began to think about the boating job. There were no gloves of any sort on the cruiser, it proved. I hadn't thought to bring any. Moreover, as the fish was worked closer and closer to the moment at which I was to seize the leader, lean over, grab it, heave the sail aboard and stun it with a milk bottle I had collected from the galley, another series of thoughts entered my head.

The moment of boating a sailfish, even in calm weather, is not unattended by small perils. There was a mate, for example, who some years ago, leaned out to execute this maneuver just as the sailfish decided to try a final desperate leap. The fish jumped—and stabbed the mate clear through the abdomen.

There was another would-be sail boater—up the Florida coast—who had the same experience but, in his case, the fish had stabbed him through the eye and into the brain.

These thoughts disturbed me. I began to wish the fish better luck. But Mildred got it up alongside. Gingerly—and barehanded—I took hold of the leader. At that instant, to my great relief, the leader, which proved to be rusty, snapped. I commiserated with the disappointed Mildred. Technically,

33

since I'd grabbed the leader, she had caught her fish even though she didn't have it to show, so I suggested that we go on in.

Larry, however, was all for more fishing. Resignedly, I sat back to watch baits. And with some trepidation I soon saw another sail behind Larry's flickering strip of fish belly. Larry reacted with great violence and excitement. I prayed that he might miss, but he didn't. In no time he was sweating and panting and his reel was snarling as a goodish sail took·line. And in no time (it seemed to me, though it was half an hour or more) I came again to the desperate exigency of bare-handed boating.

I grabbed the leader and looked down. There, a yard or so underwater, swimming hard and getting nowhere because I hung on, was the sailfish. Tentatively, I pulled. He came up a foot. I pulled again. He came another foot, and another, and there was his bill—exposed in the air at the water line, for me to grab. The water line, however, was heaving up and down a yard or so. Everyone on board was tensely watching me. And I was tensely watching the fish.

Cautiously, I bent over, and near lost my balance, and bent farther and made a swipe. I had him. I heaved again, bringing him along, threshing wildly now. I grabbed his bill with both hands and pressed him against the gunwale. I was sensible of something wrong in my hands, but I hung on while Larry raised the milk bottle and put the fish out of business. Then I looked at my hands. There was no skin left on the palm of either one, just a sort of combination bruise and tear which

34

was bleeding profusely. I have never since boated a sailfish without gloves.

But it was sailfishing, even more than tuna fishing, which turned ocean angling into the great sport, and big business, it is today. With the discovery that this fish could be hooked by dropping back, rather than striking immediately after it hit, the rush began. What had been an almost uncatchable nuisance—a fish that spoiled baits and seemed impossible to hook, a fish that broke up the tackle used by sportsmen a generation ago—turned into a spectacular fighter that a husky ten-year-old could manage to boat.

The sailfish was, and is, abundant—even though many men have spent their two-week vacation, year after year, trying vainly to get one. A spectacular battler, he also makes a spectacular mount to put above a den fireplace. His meat is good to eat, when smoked, although it is illegal to take him for this purpose in Florida waters.

Old sailfish hands usually return him alive to the sea after a tussle with him, just as old-timers return tarpon. The excitement, the relish, of his quest depends not so much on his strength and his leaping proclivities as on his variety. For, in the case of a sailfish—even more, I think, than in the case of his bigger cousin, the marlin—once he is sighted, anything probably will happen.

Some days sailfish will seem to be so ravenous that they strike like trout, not bothering to stun their quarry first. On other days they will follow baits for miles, hitting at them, but not devouring them, yet picking up the trail again when the

35

disappointed angler reels in and starts to troll again. Sometimes they lie on the surface with their big dorsal fins standing up like real sails, paper-dry in the sunshine. On these occasions they may come rushing for your bait along the surface, even jumping as they do so, like dolphin. On other days they may not appear at all and their strike will be made from the depths.

Some sails fight like 'cudas—shaking their heads, ragging the bait, rattling the angler's shoulders. Some, like wahoo, simply streak about just below the surface, sizzling the line and keeping the reel in a high song until they are spent. And still others sound immediately, like grouper, to the sea bottom, where they remain, plunging doggedly about. A few neither race nor sound, bulldog nor sulk, but expend their whole enormous store of energy within a few dozen yards of the boat in one immense, pinwheeling leap after another.

Naturally, the first tackle used on sailfish was heavy and cumbersome, but, as the lore of the species grew, anglers tried constantly lighter tackle. The lighter the gear used, the more sporting the catch. I myself spent some seasons taking sailfish and white marlin with a 6/o reel filled with six-thread, or eighteen-pound-test, line, on a rod tip of just under four ounces. Excepting for the fact that I had more line—several hundred yards—I have seen many men fishing for smallmouth black bass with tackle as heavy, and even heavier.

On such tackle, the sailfish presents several stimulating problems. It is difficult, to begin with, to drive in the hook when any yank of more than eighteen pounds will snap the line. The drag cannot be set very high, for the same reason, and a sailfish can pull against a twelve-pound drag, say, indefinitely. Indeed, it would probably be impossible to take sail-fish on such gear if they had the sense to select a straight course and simply stay on it until they had taken out all the line—at which point, by one more tail stroke and muscle spasm, they could break same. Fortunately for the angler, however, sail-fish usually aren't that bright.

Occasionally, however, I have stood by, helpless, while a hooked sail simply took off every inch of my six-thread and went on afterward, trailing some long fragment of it in the sea. But, with a five-ounce rod tip and nine-thread line—still very light tackle—any angler, even the novice, is equipped to do business with a sail. Light tackle, in my opinion, is best for the novice, owing to the fact that heavy gear gives him the false impression that he can exert any amount of pressure at any time on the sea-smashing fish. The result of that impression is, frequently, a sudden heave which pops the heaviest line and leaves the angler *sans* fish, and perhaps flat on the deck be-sides.

People sometimes ask me if, in my opinion, fishing isn't in-humane. They think of a fish as a sensitive and affectionate creature like themselves and the sight of a hook reminds them of how it hurt when they ran the sewing machine over their thumb. They do not realize that what a hooked fish feels is probably rage and possibly fear but certainly not pain in our sense. Any angler has too often watched an injured fish, torn, slashed, gutted, tailless—calmly go back to its school and begin feeding, unaware of more than inconvenience—to make the mistake of thinking that fish suffer cruelly.

Fish live on fish, which may be a scary business for fishes, but it is not painful. And fish fight each other, especially sails. I have often caught one that has been repeatedly reamed clear through by the bill of another sailfish. The round holes had healed and scarred over. I have caught them with fresh holes in their flanks. And once I saw a sailfish caught in which the broken bill of an antagonist was still buried.

I am also often asked how it is that I find fun in going out, year after year, to catch the same fishes in the same fashion and then—to turn them loose again. Part of the answer, as I've implied, is that fishing is never twice the same. The sea itself has no two identical days. But the angler, if he has the time to spend and the interest, generally becomes, in the end, less angler and more naturalist.

And I have known dozens who gradually became sea students. For, though we think of the world as well explored, most of the sea is terra incognita. The habits of sea creatures are poorly known. The sail—familiar as he is—is enigmatical. Where does he spawn? Nobody can tell you exactly. How? Who knows?

Nowadays, when Mrs. Wylie and I go fishing, we are apt to go in a glass-bottomed boat and, sometimes, without one hook or line or rod on board. We go to look. Over the coral reefs, along the inside ranges of the sailfish, we drift and stare and study.

Maybe we'll learn something new about fishes this way. Maybe we'll even spot a new fish.

The admirable barracuda

"Hey!" called a friend of mine to a casting companion, "look behind you!"

The gentleman so addressed stopped wading in the gin-clear water of Florida Bay. Shore was a good two hundred yards distant. His salmon fly lay unattended on the placid surface. He looked back—and turned pale.

Behind him, between him and the narrow beach, three dark, torpedo-shaped bodies lay motionless. Under a few inches of water, they looked dark; not black, but greenish-brown and each was at least four feet long. Perspiration burst upon the face of the fly-casting gentleman but his inward sensation was one of chill, for the three fish were specimens of *Sphyraena,* the Great Barracuda of Florida and the West Indies.

By and by the gentleman, who had been wading and casting for smaller breeds of fishes, spoke shakily to my friend "What'll I do?"

"Walk along a bit and see how they react."

"Don't they hit things that move?"

"Well—you can't just stand there, the rest of your life."

The gentleman walked forward, nervously. The 'cudas, without much show of effort, swam along, keeping their distance. The fact that they kept their distance encouraged the fly caster. Gradually he altered the direction of his steps, curving them in toward shore. The 'cudas, like a trio of private eyes in a mystery story, tailed him right up to the place where the sea margin became so shallow that their dorsal fins showed. The gentleman made the beach. He sat down and tremulously lighted a cigarette.

He had had a narrow escape from a hideous fate, he felt. The "tiger of the sea," the "terror of the sea," the "most dangerous" of the true fishes, the "fish that is worse than any shark," had stalked him. And not just one, but three of them! If they'd been a little hungrier, he thought, or if he'd made too much splash as he walked carefully on the marly bottom, curtains for him! A bullet-like acceleration and the fearsome teeth would have clamped on his leg muscles, tearing out chunks as their lunges carried them beyond his legs. Maybe he'd have made shore after that and maybe not but, in any

40

case, he'd have been a cripple for life. So he believed.

But my friend, an old-timer in Florida, came ashore, too. He was laughing. "Scare you?"

"Scare me!" The voice squeaked.

"They won't hurt you! Barracuda have a bad reputation they don't deserve. I've walked the flats, casting, a hundred times, with one, or two, or a whole school of 'cudas tagging after me."

"Yeah?" Doubt in the tone.

"Yeah. Fish are full of curiosity. Make a funny noise and they're as likely to investigate as to scram. Wade the flats, and they tool along behind you just for fun. Come on. Let's go fishing."

My friend waded back into the sea and the 'cudas lined up behind him. He ignored them. Nothing happened. . . .

What's the *truth* about the great barracuda? *Is* he dangerous to man, as some say? As even the dictionary says?

Well . . . yes and no. The answer's complicated, and fascinating.

The Miami Beach Chamber of Commerce won't like the next pieces of that answer. But they happen to be illustrative.

A good many years ago another friend of mine was on his way to Miami from New York by steamer when he made the acquaintance of a very sad-seeming, middle-aged man. My friend eventually learned the cause of the stranger's sorrow. He was on his way to Florida to bury his son. His son had been swimming somewhere off the beach, near shore, when a barracuda had hit him, taking his arm off at the shoulder.

41

Shock, and the loss of blood before he could get the hemor-
rhage staunched, had cost his life. One bite, one arm, and
death.

There used to be an elevator operator in one of the Miami
Beach hotels who wore a pinned sleeve. A good swimmer, he
had tried one day to swim across then-pretty, now-polluted
Biscayne Bay, a stretch of water which lies between Miami
and Miami Beach. About halfway out, he'd been hit by what
he is sure was a barracuda. It came faster than any shallow-
water shark, he reported. He had a glimpse of "silver sides and
black splotches" as it struck him. He lost so much of the muscle
tissue of his arm that amputation was necessary. However, a
boat was accompanying him, so he was pulled out of the water
immediately. The bite was low enough to leave room for a
tourniquet. He lost an arm but not his life.

Was the old-timer, who advised that it is harmless to have
a bevy of barracudas following you as you wade around, dead-
wrong? Or was he right?

Is the presence of the big 'cuda near a bathing beach so
rare as to make the risk of meeting one negligible? Is it, as
they say, a thousand times safer to swim off south Florida than
to cross any street at a busy intersection in the rush hour? Obviously, it is safe. Such frightful accidents as the two reported
above are almost as scarce as damage done by meteors and far
scarcer than injury by, say, lightning. But that is not owing to
the rarity of 'cudas inshore.

Several years ago, at a cabana club where we spent part of
nearly every day, some of us took to wearing goggles in order
to observe the small, bright tropical fish which inhabited the

groines. "Groines" are long walls extending into the sea to hold the sand and to encourage the deposit of additional sand. They are made of piles driven deep and bolted to beams, or of corrugated iron. Barnacles encrust them and gaudy fishes, an inch or two in length, swarm in their waterlogged recesses. By wearing goggles and swimming under water three or four feet down alongside the groines, one is able to study that beautiful, miniature world.

Also, barracudas. The first one I saw was about four feet from the round glass face of my goggles—and about four feet long. I had finished an underwater stroke and taken hold of a rough piling to anchor myself for a look at lesser fauna. I was, in other words, merely floating there, a few feet down. So was the barracuda. His gills worked. His mouth was slightly open. I could see, with an extreme clarity, the ivory-colored teeth which give him his reputation. Each tooth, in a fish of that size, is about like one of your own canine teeth. I could also see the 'cuda's eyes which were fixed on me with an unreadable expression. He just stayed there, doing nothing.

I pushed myself back a ways. He came toward me exactly the same distance. So I reversed and went toward him. He retreated—the same distance. That encouraged me—a little. I let go and swam, still under water, toward the fish. He gave me what I think of as a dirty look, turned calmly, and was gone like an arrow. I then came up for air, which I needed.

Subsequently, I ran into numerous 'cudas along the groines. Occasionally, I have seen their dark shapes streaking amongst a horde of swimmers. It is known generally to life-guards and to anglers that barracudas hang around groines,

43

probably to feed on the small fish there. Yet millions of people swim with those 'cudas and years go by without anybody getting bitten. Sunburn causes a hundred times as much pain, suffering and even real trouble. And if any one does get bitten, the 'cuda is almost invariably blamed although, perhaps, it wasn't a barracuda at all. A shark, perhaps.

Even a little shark, a sand shark, a nurse shark, one of the small black-tips that frequent shallow water. They are called "harmless" and time was when I treated them with contempt. Last year, however, a friend of mine, a former parachute trooper who relaxes these days by goggle-fishing on the larger and more formidable reefs, harpooned one of those "little" sharks and tried to grab it. The shark cut around, grabbed him—and he got a nasty bite. Last year, too, a scientist at work in the "pens" of the Lerner Marine Laboratory in Bimini tangled with a "baby" shark and received a bite that meant a tourniquet, plasma, a fast trip by air to a mainland hospital and many days in mending. So I have grown cautious about "harmless," "baby" sharks of fifty or a hundred pounds! Baby lion cubs are often docile. But sharks. . . . ?

And yet, the 'cuda isn't exonerated.

We'd been bottom-fishing all day with Leo Johnson, one of the most sea-sophisticated guides in all the Florida Keys. Twilight descended over the tranquil Bay, the thousands of square miles of knee-deep, neck-deep, fish-teeming water. The last ruddy-gold of the sunset dyed the surface and turned near-by islands a theatrical green. My hands, as is common with anglers' hands, were a bit fishy. Idly, I reached one overboard to wash in the warm salt water.

"For God's sake," Leo cried, "don't do that, Phil!"

"Why?" My hand came out, fast.

Leo grinned a little. "Twice, just about this time of day, after sitting still as we've been doing, when I dipped my oars, big 'cudas charged from nowhere, hit the blades, and broke the oars. It's the sudden splash that brings 'em, I guess—like the one you just made. They're lying around—see the riffle—and hit before they stop to figure whether it's an oar blade or some damned writer's good left hand."

It takes a lot of power to bite a chunk out of an oar blade.

Barracudas have that power. If the reader can bear with more personal testimony, it will be shown *how much* steam they have.

Let us go back twenty years, to the time when an old fresh-water angler, a brook-trout man, a black-bass, pike and muskie fisherman, was getting his first taste of what happens when you drop a line in the ocean. We're on board the charterboat *Fish Hawk*, out of Miami, en route to Key Largo. Sailfish baits are skittering. Tom Frazure, the skipper, puts out a center line—a heavy line, a line like sash cord, with a wire leader and a big spoon. It is made fast to a cleat on the gunwale and, for a while, Tom jigs it—yanking in a yard of line and letting it drop back to give the spoon a darting, fishlike motion. By and by Tom turns to some other task and our novice ocean angler decides to continue jigging the center line.

As an old fresh-water man, he has done this before. He is unalarmed by any possibility. So, to give himself a more comfortable hold on the line, he takes a half-dozen turns around his hand. There he stands, at the low stern, jigging away and inextricably attached to the heavy line—a moron and imbecile, if there ever was one—named Wylie. Philip Wylie.

Comes a strike. None of your rainbow trout, pickerel or even muskie-type strikes. Our halfwit hero's arm is nearly yanked out of its socket. He is spun about and hurled against the stern. He exerts all his strength but he loses his balance nevertheless and is hauled toward the sea where the propeller is furiously churning. A mighty force is acting upon him. But, as he shoots overboard, he grabs a stern-post which, luckily, happens to be in his path. His free hand takes a death grip. His torso, hips, feet fly out and down. His ankles hit the water and he bends up his knees, to keep the "wheel" from chewing up his tootsies. His right arm still points seaward, straight and tense, as the big 'cuda that dragged him across the stern now tries to drag him the rest of the way. A quick mate and a horrified wife grab the inboard residue of the fisherman. After a tug-of-war, they get him back into the cockpit. Line is unwound from the bruised hand; the strained arm is freed; a glove-wearing mate brings in the fish. Forty-six pounds of barracuda that nearly caused the undoing of a hundred and sixty pounds of nitwit.

Since that day, I have *never* wound line around my hand, finger, or any other part of my anatomy. Not when there was a hook on it and the hook was in salt water!

So much for the power of the 'cuda, his reputation and the various menacing or deadly experiences that are had with him. How do they add up? Is it true that 'cudas hit only moving objects? Is it true, as the Bahama natives assert, that they hit white men but never black? Is a good suntan a protection for a white swimmer? Are 'cudas "man-*eaters*"?

After twenty years of personal experience and close observation, after discussions with hundreds of guides and scores of Bahama natives, after much technical reading and careful inquiry among scientists, I *still* have very few positive ideas about the behavior of the great barracuda in respect to man. It isn't news that 'cudas sometimes bite men—and women, and children. They do. But it may have been news to most readers that 'cudas are often plentiful in regions patronized by bathers and that bites in such regions are rare, almost nil. Here, then, are some reasonable generalities, to which, I fear, exceptions may be possible:

A wading or swimming man has little to fear from a following or loitering 'cuda; the fish probably hasn't anything better to do that day than to hang around watching how people behave. Goggle-fishermen and Bahama and West Indian natives (along with the guides, attendants and scientists who wade and swim in the barracuda-thronged "pens" of the American Museum of Natural History's Bimini Lab) are accustomed to going about their business in the midst of 'cudas. They are usually careful not to make too much splash, careful not to chase, prod or excite their sabre-toothed associates; otherwise, they take no precautions.

I have swum cheek-by-jowl with big barracudas, not entirely comfortably, but in no panic. I've seen Angelo, a native guide in Bimini, dive for a rod dropped overboard in twenty feet of 'cuda-infested water. No harm. Captain Eddie Wall,

47

the famed skipper of the yacht *Playmate,* fears the sharp, slicing dorsal of the eight-inch surgeonfish more than the wolflike jaws of any 'cuda.

It may be a 'cuda is more likely to hit a white man, simply because a colored person or a tan one resembles a water-soaked board or a stone, a white one looks like edible fish. Certainly the sudden splash of a hand (or an oar!) or perhaps of a swimmer's arm, or of a dive, courts a hit more than quiet, steady wading, or swimming, or underwater swimming.

Barracudas have no reputation (as do sharks) for attacking people "in trouble" or injured people. When they do bite, it isn't because their victim is already in bad condition. And I have never heard of an authentic case of a gang or school of barracudas devouring anybody; with sharks, it's different.

What *may* be the case, in the rather uncommon matter of 'cuda bite, is this: an individual fish acts in an uncommon fashion. For fish, contrary to popular belief, are intensely individual. The brilliant and bold Dr. Kinsey, before he undertook to show the immense variation in human sex behavior, made some contributions to science in the matter of gall wasps. These lowly insects, he demonstrated, do not, as individuals, invariably and perfectly pursue the pattern laid down by their instincts. Now and again an individual gall wasp does something on his own, something not in the gall-wasp rule book. It may be the same with barracudas; here and there a single fish will hit a man when the next million of the same size in the same spot would let the man alone.

Contrarywise, a common form of fish behavior is what possibly affords Florida's bathers their main protection. It was found years ago, at the fabulous Marineland, that fish are very "property-conscious." A little fish, arriving first at a good hole in the coral, may be permitted to live in it and hang around it by a much larger fish that would normally prey on the small one. There is a sort of "safe-at-home-base" custom at work here. Perhaps the 'cudas which come up on the beaches take the instinctual view that swimmers were there first and own the joint—that they are the intruders, the ones obliged to mind their manners. At any rate, if you swim at Miami Beach, you needn't worry about 'cudas. They may be there; the danger from them is next to nil.

Before the matter of the 'cuda's danger is dropped for a brighter aspect of that interesting fish, one more item should be discussed. Great fear is often shown by novice anglers when a 'cuda is boated. His bad name and his manifestly wicked teeth cause persons to imagine he is capable of attack on dry land—of striking like a rattlesnake. Not so. Quite a few people *have* been scratched, raked, even badly cut or bitten by boated barracudas. But that is not because the fish went after them; it happens when they, carelessly, get part of an arm, a hand, or foot, or a finger between the 'cuda's jaws. Naturally, if he has a chance, he'll clamp down. Hooked, ashore, he may even gnash his teeth on general principles. *So will any fish.* Any fish with teeth or sharp jaws, sharp or pointed fins, or barbed gill-rakes offers the same hazard, exactly. John Smedberg, for many years mate on Harold Schmitt's famed *Neptune,* wears a scar on his arm made when a wahoo (a kind of super-mackerel) threw a hook, jumped in the air, and came down, unfortunately, jaws-first against Smedberg's arm.

Some fish

In boating a 'cuda it is necessary, merely, to take ordinary precautions. Not little ones. Gaff every big one. But don't reach into his mouth to loosen the hook, or for any other reason. Don't decide to test the sharpness of his teeth by feeling them while he's still alive. Use pliers, a knife, a hard shake of the fish, a stick, or other remote-control means to free the hook. If you can't free it, cut the leader and put on a new hook. Get the other back by surgery when the 'cuda is dead. Those rules apply for the little snappers as much as for tigers of the sea; snappers can bite, too!

As a menace-to-man, the barracuda is to be reckoned with, even if his terrible reputation represents considerable exaggeration. However, it is as *a sport or game fish* that the 'cuda deserves a new reputation. In that category, he is to be admired and sought after.

A barracuda will hit any known kind of bait that moves, and he will sometimes even take the bait of a still fisherman. Any size 'cuda will hit any bait of feasible size for him. Indeed, a ten-pound 'cuda will not hesitate, if in the mood, to slice at (and slice in two!) a six-pound bonefish trolled for blue marlin. A 'cuda will take a trout fly. A plug. A grasshopper. A feather. A trolling spoon. Practically anything else being trolled, including a piece of cloth, or even a bare, bright hook! He will hit a cut strip of bait, a live fish used as bait (especially that!) or a whole, deceased fish. He is exceedingly unparticular. And that, from the angler's standpoint, is an advantage. Furthermore, his range is vast—from the great Gulf Stream to the lowliest salt backwater.

When hooked, a 'cuda will often put on as good a show,

pound for pound, as his far more famous game-fish colleagues. His runs are very fast, long, sweeping and extremely powerful. (Note the earlier account of one that pulled me halfway overboard against my will, balance, and muscle.) The barracuda is also among the fish which "bulldog." A good-sized one, on light tackle, down twenty or thirty feet, slashing his head from side to side, will give the angler an astonishing kind of battle— a fast, sawing, yanking struggle to keep a tight line—and so keep the fish.

The strike of a 'cuda is nearly always sensational. The fish may sometimes be seen, a streak, a whistling cut-water, racing toward the bait. The hit itself is an explosion. One is reminded of the trajectory and blast of a rocket shot by a bazooka. Sometimes the 'cuda leaps clear and falls on the bait. Generally, however, he hits and turns at the same instant, throwing geysers of water, often hurling himself half-clear in the process. And he is, as a rule, that prize among prizes, a leaping fish. I've caught many barracudas of twenty to thirty pounds that jumped more times than many of the sailfish I've taken. High, clear and frenzied, his dark back, white belly, black-spotted silver sides rise and somersault in the sunlight. Quite a sight!

The caster, whether he uses a fly rod or plugs, will find the barracuda ideal. One does not have to go out into the rugged Gulf Stream for him. One doesn't have even to search the sometimes rough waters of the reefs. Barracudas like bays, coves, island shores, salt ponds, salt creeks, the edges of salt marshes. A twenty-pounder may be spotted in a mere ten inches of water. And that's another fascination of the breed:

51

the angler can *hunt* for him, rowing, paddling, poling, wading —and holding his fire until he sees one of the submarine-shaped behemoths, of a suitable size for his gear, lying motion-less in a spot where the fisherman can make a good cast and conduct the strategy of his scrap afterward, in selected ter-ritory. A man with a trout rod probably won't have much luck if he casts his fly to a ten-pounder. But a man with a plug-casting outfit of the sort designed for black-bass fishing, if he has a hundred yards of ten-pound test line, could toss his Bob-bling Benny, Dalmation Dipper, or Leaping Leona at a twenty-pounder in the expectation that, after a hair-raising conflict, he might win. Might not, too.

In some ways, the 'cuda ought to be classed as a "prince" of light-tackle Florida game fishes for casters. His abundance, his voracity, the number of locales he patronizes, his edibility (of which more later) and particularly the versatile violence of the fight he gives, should assure him a title. Unfortunately, his vices and alleged vices have hurt his name. And until quite recently he was not, as a rule, taken by methods suitable to his supporting nature. People have caught barracudas for generations, centuries. But they have caught them, usually, on heavy hand lines or on rods and rigs designed for down-boring reef fish such as amberjack and groupers. Only in the last ten years or so has any sizable number of people realized that sail-fish-tackle itself should be light. And only in the same short period have anglers in numbers commenced to find out what they can do in the sea with the gear they'd hitherto used for steelheads, salmon, muskies, black bass, and pike.

The 'cuda is, actually, a pikelike fish. A muskielike fish.

The admirable barracuda

A remote cousin of those breeds, with the added jet-propulsion needed for survival in the sea. But it is not necessary to go after him with such tackle as might be needed to hoist a hundred-pound grouper out of a coral cave. The hooked 'cuda won't sound and hide; he'll fight it out with you in the water, on or near the surface generally, and in the air. He, too, *can* weigh a hundred pounds, or more, but monsters of that size are rare and a fifty-pound 'cuda is a big one. You don't need a tank to hunt pheasant; you don't need a crane and a cable to catch barracudas. Light tackle is the thing—a nine-thread line will do for the biggest one you'll ever hook in your life *if* you have yards enough of nine-thread on your reel. Say, five hundred yards, for that record breaker. And records, in the 'cuda category, are constantly being broken.

Below are the current world records for the various tackle sizes recognized by the International Game Fish Association; the figures of each "class" represent maximum breaking strain of the line used:

Barracuda records

	Pounds	Length	Girth	
ALL TACKLE:	103¼	5'6"	31¼"	Bahama Islands, 1932, C. E. Benet, on 80-pound test
12-pound:	27	4'9"	17½"	Lagos, Nigeria, May 24, 1950, J. N. Zarpas
20-pound:	58¼	5'4½"	26"	Craig, Florida, May 11, 1946, B. L. Clark
30-pound:	44	4'4"	25¾"	Fowey Light, Florida, June 10, 1945, J. Van Wickle

53

Some fish

	Pounds	Length	Girth	
50-pound:	59½	4'11"	25½"	Key Largo, Florida, Sept. 6, 1948, Charlotte Sibole
80-pound:	See All-Tackle Record			

Women's records

ALL TACKLE: See the Charlotte Sibole 59½-pound catch which is also the 50-pound record for both men and women.

	Pounds	Length	Girth	
12-pound:	22¼	4'5"	49"	Bimini, B.W.I., May 1, 1950, Mrs. Louis Marron
20-pound:	No record			
30-pound:	32	4'7½"	32½"	Long Key, Florida, May 22, 1949, Mrs. E. Johnson
50-pound:	See Women's All Tackle			

How would you like to have one of those records? Well, what's to hinder you? Pick out your favorite *kind* of tackle, your favorite *style* of fishing, take note of the present world record, spend your next vacation in Florida, the Bahamas, the West Indies, where barracudas of all sizes and vast appetite are numerous, and see if you can't "knock off" the present holder of the world's record in the class you've chosen. The biggest ones are yet to be caught! As for abundance—many times, around the base of one or another of the lighthouses along the Florida east coast, I've seen *thousands upon thousands* of 'cudas lying like schooled minnows—all facing the same way—torpedo-ominous, ranging from ten—to sixty-pounders!

Barracudas are perfectly good to eat.

That statement, I feel sure, will result in howls of protest unless it is amplified. And its amplification opens up still another mystery of one of the sea's most baffling fish. Put it this way: There are people, known to me and including me, who have eaten barracudas, male and female, in various regions, at all different seasons, with enjoyment and no ill effect. There are others who claim to have been made violently ill by eating barracuda.

Science isn't entirely helpful here either. I have read a treatise by an ichthyologist in which it was suggested that possibly female 'cudas, when full of roe, generate a toxic substance as a protection against attack by other fish—which, *maybe*, makes some people ill. Other wizards point out that certain persons are allergic to all fish, or to certain fish. Hence those who claim to have been made ill by 'cuda meat may have been merely allergic. Another suggestion offered by year-round 'cuda-consumers is that if the meat makes anybody ill, it is because it is kept unrefrigerated too long and has spoiled. Thus (they hold) it is not the fact that they ate *'cuda,* but *spoiled fish,* which causes their distress.

The meat is good-looking, white, flaky, savory and tasty. It sometimes finds its way to fish markets and restaurants, under other names, of which "sea pike" is one (though "sea pike" may mean the equally excellent and utterly innocent robalo or snook), and I have never heard of an outbreak of "sea pike" poisoning.

I myself suspect that most barracuda "poisoning" is psychosomatic—and often wonder why psychologists (hard-pressed to demonstrate their new knowledge) don't refer oftener to the *psychology of food*.

The matter of eating the barracuda is a case in point. If you give a man a "chicken sandwich" he will eat it with gusto, no doubt, and without harm. If you give him the same thing, a day later, and he eats it and you then both tell him and prove to him that both sandwiches were made of the meat of a rattlesnake, he may become very ill from his second sandwich even though the first didn't upset him. That illness, obviously, rises from his mind, not his insides. So it may be with barracudas. People eating them unknowingly and told about it afterward, or people eating them nervously and worrying afterward, may *make themselves* ill.

And they may worry, of course, for two "reasons"—because of the rumor that the meat has sometimes been toxic, or because of revulsion over eating the meat of anything that "eats" people. The latter sentiment, of course, is rather silly, on two counts: a 'cuda that has had a bite of *genus homo* is very, very rare; and chickens and pigs, to name just two popular food animals, do the same, on occasion, if given the chance.

Indeed, the cases of human pig bite, together with injury or death due to it, probably outnumber the 'cuda disasters a thousand to one. Yet people don't usually grow pale in the presence of porkers. And millions of farmers enter pigpens calmly every day. Only once in a great while does a pig attack a person.

So my net testimony is pro-'cuda. The barracuda is a

handsome, gallant, game and food fish which, on rare occasion, has taken advantage of a man invading his element. This, in turn, has given him an overblown reputation for aggression.

People have been stabbed while boating sailfish; they have had their boats wrecked by marlin; they have had their arms and legs broken by tarpon that jumped aboard or were taken aboard too soon. But nobody holds a shuddersome view of sailfish, marlin or tarpon owing to that!

After twenty years of swimming over the reefs and in the open seas where the Great Barracuda lives, after catching thousands by a dozen methods, and after the same number of years devoted to beach and surf activities in Florida and the Bahamas, I can testify that I never saw a 'cuda even *make a pass* at a person. I am convinced that their "menacing" way of lurking about is merely a manifestation of curiosity. And I have come to suspect that at least some of the damage attributed to barracudas has been the work of sharks, even small sharks, that hit hard and rush away, showing only a flash of white.

But I could be wrong. So I observe a few rules. I don't stick my hands or feet suddenly into tropical salt water, as I do into fresh. I don't dive, except in pools and along beaches where swimming is a constant event. I take care, when a 'cuda is boated, to avoid his jaws. And I never put my hand in his mouth unless and until I am certain he is dead. If a really big 'cuda comes in on a beach where I'm swimming, and hangs around, I get the kids and others out and throw rocks at him till he beats it. Sometimes, instead of rocks, I cast a bass plug, in which case I sometimes remove that 'cuda from the sea for good and all. I eat 'cuda unhesitatingly, though the choice of

57

food in tropical seas is so varied that a day's fishing usually provides species I prefer to barracuda.

Respect, rather than fear, is indicated by this sporty fellow with the bad name. If you were to watch the students of marine biology, at the University of Miami—young men and pretty girls—year after year don diving helmets and descend to the coral gardens to make first-hand surveys, you would be reassured about 'cudas. For as the students stand, sit and plod about amongst the weird scenes—the lunar rocks, the purple and yellow fans, the swarms of fishes bright as Christmas-tree balls—you'd see the 'cudas, too, hanging around, watching, following, retreating. Not bothering anybody. Perhaps they're just studying *terrestrial biology*. Who knows?

And that's a question which arises wherever the sea is concerned, or the fishes in it: *Who knows?* That's why the quest goes on and why, perhaps, some day a more informed amateur naturalist than I may be able to tell exactly *why* it is that, once in a great while, a 'cuda bites a man, and perhaps why *sometimes* a bite of 'cuda makes a man sick. Until then, the sportsman is safe in dealing with the barracuda for what he is: the biggest, ruggedest, flashiest and fightingest pike in the water world.

A marlin is a fighting fish

All marlin are mean and most marlin are insane. They are big fish. In some branches of the family, a thousand pounds is merely a respectable adulthood. Apparently no one, fishing fairly and squarely with sports tackle, has taken a marlin of that size in the Atlantic; but commercial fishermen off Cuba, with deep sets and ropes, do it as a matter of course. And several famed sportsmen have broken the "G"-mark, lately, in the Pacific, off Chile.

The marlin looks like a heavy-duty sailfish—sans sail. A thicker, huskier animal, gun-metal above, chrome-silver below, ornamented with iridescent blues and lavenders, beefed up around the shoulders and possessed of a wilder eye than any bull. The sailfish's bill is a rapier. The marlin's is a policeman's billy with the added feature of a point like that of an ice ax. But it was natural that, after never-satisfied man had learned to catch the pinwheeling sail, he would raise his sights to see what could be done with rod and reel in the matter of marlin.

There are two breeds in the Atlantic—the big blue and his nephew, the smaller white marlin. Anyone who has hooked and boated the nephew will know he has been tangled in the championship class. And anyone who has even hooked a blue will remember what happened afterward with somewhat the same awe and alarm that he might recall participating in a train wreck.

People do it on purpose—even though the deed requires much hunting, as a rule, for marlin, like all great, voracious game animals, are not abundant—and even though the finding of a marlin in the sea, the luring of said fish to the bait, and the hooking of same, by no means guarantees the catch. I ought to know. Before I actually brought my own first blue to boat, I had hooked and fought—for a longer or shorter time— eight others. And a great many years had passed between the first and the ninth.

To catch a blue marlin in the latitudes where I live, the latitudes of south Florida and Bimini, in the British Bahamas, you troll from a conventional fishing boat—one with sturdy outriggers and stout tackle. The lightest line recommended for the beginner is twenty-four-thread, which breaks under a strain of seventy-two pounds. But thirty-nine-thread, with a breaking strain of 117 pounds, is better. And most people start out with fifty-four-thread line. It is a good idea for the angler to know his own breaking strain, besides. For it generally takes an hour or two—or maybe three or four—to lick a blue marlin with rod and reel. It will be amongst the more onerous periods of the angler's life. A period filled with excitement—one during which carelessness can be extremely dangerous. The sport is not recommended for persons who are unsure of the state of their hearts, backs, biceps and general morale. More than one man who fancied himself in adequate condition has died of heart failure after an encounter with a marlin.

The bait for sailfish is a mullet, a balao, or a cut strip of fish belly the length of a man's hand. The bait most prized for marlin in these latitudes is a bonefish, whole—a two- to five-pounder, with six- and eight-pounders acceptable. The bonefish itself is regarded by tens of thousands of anglers as the finest light-tackle quarry the sea affords. But, in the marlin quest, a bonefish is only bait. That gives some idea.

To give the rest of the idea would require a convocation of all the anglers who have ever—by accident or deliberate intent—"hung" a blue marlin. Or a white. I can offer only what I've seen, experienced, or heard from fishermen and fishing guides whose habit is complete honesty and even understatement, a common practice amongst sports fishermen, contrary to the tired gag about their exaggerations.

Skip, then, the eight marlin that I hooked and lost. Skip many years of luckless fishing. And skip back ten years or so to a day off the Florida Keys when, with my wife and some

61

friends, we were taking dead aim for blue marlin in the *Sea Queen,* captained by Art Wills. I had heard, from Pan American pilots, that at a certain point off the Keys, in a certain time of year (and don't bother writing to ask where and when; it's still my secret), great numbers of marlin could be seen from the air. We were down there, then, on a warm and windy day—blue sky, Caribbean clouds phalanxing overhead to make a regular and welcome interruption of the tropical sunshine—with two big rods and reels in the fighting chairs and two bonefish banging along astern on lines that led from the outriggers.

Every time these baits were yanked from a wave top they came down with splash enough for a normal good strike. These splashes brought myriad false alerts to our friends, who were novices. To make our tenseness greater, we occasionally saw dead or injured mackerel. It looked as if some big fishes had been feeding in mackerel schools—fishes that clubbed first with their bills and then turned to feed. Marlin, for instance. It looked, that is to say, as if there was substance in the tip I'd had from the pilots.

This substance became reality when the mate, at the controls on top of the cabin, suddenly yelled, "Here he comes— your side, Mr. Wylie!"

And there, indeed, he came. I had a glimpse of a black bill slashing in the purple water behind my bait. I saw the high-standing dorsal. Underneath it was a frighteningly big shadow. A mouth opened—it seemed as big as a coal scuttle. My bonefish was engulfed. The line whipped out of the clothespin high on the outrigger and the big "V" of slack fell into the sea. This slack gives the marlin (as it does the sailfish) the impression that he has stunned his quarry and furnishes him time enough, thereafter, as the boat moves on, to devour what he has hit.

I leaped into the fighting chair and buckled on the harness—just in time. The slack came up and I struck, not with my arms, as one does for sailfish, but with my back and shoulders, across which stretched the broad belt of a harness, fixed to the reel. I struck three times. The marlin began responding immediately. I wished that some of my trout-angling friends who are accustomed to a run across a thirty-foot pool and under a two-foot waterfall could have been there. For my marlin beelined away from the boat, at top speed and without stopping or turning, for five hundred straight yards!

When he did turn, he turned up. At a distance of a little more than a quarter of a mile, he dived into the air, twisting, writhing, falling, throwing spray like an air-launched torpedo and catapulting back into the atmosphere again. Six jumps and he decided to try the straight pull again. The skipper cut the boat around and gave chase. We ran for a mile or more, neck and neck. Or possibly, in that furious mile, I got back a little line. Unfortunately, from the standpoint of the marlin, this one decided on a new course. He took off at right angles, and then I did gain line.

In ten minutes—or fifteen—or twenty—he stopped dead. For five more minutes he lay beneath the tossing surface of the indigo sea and merely shook his head. Every time he shook it, I was lifted out of my seat—and, of course, dropped back with all the force that gravity invests in the sudden release of support. The marlin leaped again. For fifty yards or so he ran

63

along on his tail, throwing a wake like an outboard racer and eying us bitterly. Then he bored straight down.

The *Sea Queen* was ten miles offshore; the Gulf Stream ran deep there. But this particular marlin sounded until he hit the bottom. That fact we were able to prove later for, on his belly, were deep scratches from the coral reef.

Fighting a marlin that has sounded is something like trying to keep a mineshaft elevator from falling deeper into its pit with a winch that slips. The strain is incessant, the weight tremendous, and whenever you reel a few precious yards of line onto the spindle, something gives, and down the fish goes again, taking all you gained, or more, or—if you are lucky and the fish is tiring, perhaps a little less. I have hooked marlin that went down a couple of thousand feet and stayed there, dogging around. I have fought them there for hours, through thunder storms that snapped down lightning on the surrounding sea, through stinging rain squalls, into darkness—fought them, and lost them there, when the line finally broke or some sharp edge of reef cut it in two.

This marlin, destined to be my first, gave up hunting for safety in the pitch-dark ocean abyss after half an hour. He began a return to the surface that beat my fastest efforts to reel and came out within fifty yards of the boat. Here you will begin to see why I said that marlin are insane.

The big fish reconnoitered us by means of a few fast-breaking leaps and by greyhounding around our stern. When I got a tight line on him again, he charged the boat.

There is a considerable dispute amongst not only anglers but scientists as to whether marlin take this rare step on purpose or merely in their random, wild way of getting about. I hold with the "on purpose" school. But, whether with intended malice or with mere blind indignation, the marlin poised himself on the surface, seemed to aim, and came at us like a skip bomb. He caught the *Sea Queen* squarely in the stern, too. There was a shock. The sound of sea and wind was louder than what must have been a sharp crack. For the marlin's bill point rammed into the mahogany planking of the stern and some three inches of it broke off and stayed there, like a spike, driven deep.

This outraged the fish; he lathered the sea in our immediate vicinity. Something like an hour and a half had passed, by this time. I knew I was shot. But, at lucky long last, I was battling a blue marlin that was even more spent. I began bringing him in the final, rugged hundred feet or so. The mate made a snatch at the leader wire and got it. The skipper ran to his side. Both waited for a favorable cant of the *Sea Queen* and then, suddenly, my marlin's head showed over the gunwale, his broken bill held by rippling human muscle. The despatching club was applied and in he came.

During the battle I had taken it for granted that I was fighting a monster—a five-hundred-pounder, or a bigger one. Maybe even a record-breaker. On the scales, the fish weighed 237 pounds. Not exactly a baby marlin, but a child marlin, at best.

The shattered stub of the bill protruding from the *Sea Queen's* stern attracted more attention among veteran anglers than the catch. Captain Wills cut it off flush, sanded it down and varnished it. Thereafter, for many years and until the

Some fish

Sea Queen got a new stern, he showed his passengers the dowellike plug in his mahogany—the imbedded bill of Phil Wylie's first blue. Only a few weeks before this was written, I saw the *Sea Queen* turning into Government Cut, homing to Miami after a day's charter. She was flying another marlin flag—for a white marlin, this time—but I doubt if she'd been rammed again in the battle.

Most hooked marlin don't get caught. They are too big and too furious for fishing tackle. But once in a while, a good one gets taken easily. Well, easily in a way. This happened to me the summer before last.

For three days, I'd been fishing with my daughter and a boy schoolmate off Bimini with no luck. My daughter and her pal were fifteen and their function was merely to watch the great event, but three days of sitting on a boat in fairly choppy water is monotonous, at fifteen, even when the project promises well. Toward the end of the third day they grew restless and my daughter's pal said annoyedly, "Personally, I think this is about the dullest sport I've ever heard of!"

I knew the sensation. As parent and host, I felt embarrassed. I raised my eyes and sent a silent prayer to whatever gods look after the seas. It must have been a good prayer. Ten minutes later a fair-sized blue cut across our wake at right angles, missed the bait, did a skid turn in the top of a big wave, and came back for another try.

"What was that?" my daughter asked excitedly.

"That," the mate replied calmly, "was a blue marlin, lady. Was, is, and soon will be a dead blue marlin, if we're lucky."

On his second try, the marlin nailed the bonefish. Down

66

dropped the outrigger line. I had slammed into the fighting chair; now I braced myself and struck. Apparently I yanked the bonefish out of his mouth. The marlin came back again, though. I let him have slack line, free-spooling the reel for seven or eight seconds. Then I felt him surge with the bait, and struck again. Out he whistled—350 pounds of sea-splitting, joint-cracking blue dynamite. The kids' eyes popped, the captain chortled, and the marlin threw a superfast tail-walk half-way around the boat and back again. Then he plunged under-water, rushed a few yards, and stopped.

I pumped gingerly against him and he ran a few feet. I pumped again—again he ran. This turgid behavior continued for five minutes and then, to my astonishment, I began to gain on the fish. In two more minutes, the swivel was out of water and in another moment, the mate had seized the leader wire. Eight minutes in all!

"Be careful!" Captain Harold Schmitt yelled, as he came down from the canopy. "That's a green fish! Hasn't begun to realize he's in trouble!"

But the boating of the fish proceeded. Two Bimini native boys assisted. A tail rope went round the fish. Arms heaved. In came the marlin, half filling the *Neptune*'s cockpit. Then we saw what had happened. The fish had been hooked in the eye, and resisting the hook evidently distressed it. But, as our skipper stepped forward to administer the *coup de grace,* the hook dropped out and suddenly the marlin was relieved of pain.

First, he shook the tail rope. He was entirely free not in the open sea but in the comparatively small cockpit of a fishing

67

cruiser. What happened then is difficult to describe. The two kids took shelter in the cabin and watched from there. The marlin heaved himself into the air a few times and landed on the deck with prodigious, wet thuds. He bent his tail down and up. He happened at the instant to be under a fishing chair; it was hurled high out of its bolts and moorings. Everybody grabbed a club. The boat rocked and pitched in the chop. This slid the enraged fish about in the cockpit. He jerked his head back and forth in wide, lethal arcs and his great, swinging bill constituted a threat of the first magnitude. It could have broken any leg in its way—would have. We ducked around, avoiding bill and tail, whaling at the head when we got a chance.

But it is one thing to knock a lashed marlin insensible, another to tackle a loose, flopping, bill-swinging, cockpit-filling monster. We hit it dozens of times, bashing its skin, cracking gill plates, cutting it. Blood spattered our clothes and made things so slippery it was nearly impossible to move on the deck. When, finally, we killed the brute, the place looked not as if a fish had been taken there, but as if a hand grenade had gone off. Furniture was blasted about. All five of the men on the boat were smeared with blood. Buckets were flattened and the gear was a mess.

I turned around at last to the recently bored schoolmate of my daughter. I arrested my panting and made my voice as flat as possible. "Find any excitement in that?"

I got no immediate answer. Both kids were completely speechless.

The smaller white marlin is small only by comparison.

Fish of this breed have been taken that weighed well over 150 pounds—and bigger ones, of course, have been lost. The white marlin is found year-round in the Florida-Bimini area. Here, too, he irregularly and unpredictably appears in large numbers. And in summertime, off Ocean City, Maryland, he shows up in a still greater abundance. A big white marlin will take a bait trolled for his blue uncle; and any white, if he feels in the mood, will snatch a sailfish bait. This latter fact has provided sailfishermen with an incalculable number of surprises.

The "white" marlin isn't white, of course. He resembles the blue in nearly every way; his undersides may be paler, his lavender striping is plain when he first comes out of the water, and his dorsal fin is rounded instead of pointed. Many anglers regard him as, pound-for-pound, the most rugged, enduring and formidable fish in the sea. And his comparative abundance makes it feasible to hunt for him with light tackle. A fisherman can afford to lose a few whites and hope to hook a few more without waiting down long days—and weeks interspersed through years—for another shot. Perhaps only an expert should try for a white marlin with six-thread line and only a slightly daffy expert will try him on three-thread (which has a breaking point of nine pounds), but any fairly competent fisherman with six-hundred or seven-hundred yards of nine-thread (twenty-seven-pound breaking strain) line on his reel will find himself reasonably equipped to battle any but the largest white.

Fishing for white marlin does not have quite the element of heavyweight contest that is found in blue-marlin fishing.

Some fish

But the excitement of it is intense enough for anybody. I've seen it produce a variety of strange results.

Once, when my wife and some guests and I were trolling off Miami, a heavy wind came up and the seas soon ran a good fifteen feet high. In this loud shambles of wind and water, as we started for home, I hooked a white. The subsequent combat so shook the mate that immediately after we had boated the fish, he lost his hold up topside and fell overboard. One tries at all times not to fall into the Gulf Stream. When it is running a big sea, one should never fall in. For it was a long time before we were able to get even a glimpse of the mate and a still longer time before we could get near enough to throw a line to him. All that saved his life was his ability to swim like a sea lion and the skipper's sagacity.

The mate blamed the long ducking on the fish: "I was still so darned excited I forgot to hang on!"

One year, an editor friend of mine who had read all my stories of deep-sea fishing came down to Miami and put me on the spot: "Take me out," he said, "and prove it."

I took him out and, as so often happens, we trolled all morning without a strike. The day merely grew hotter. Toward noon, my friend told me that he was going below to change into a pair of shorts. I advised him to stick to his rod and get the mate to fetch his shorts. He looked at me sneeringly and said he thought there would be plenty of time. There wasn't, of course. Soon after he vanished, a white marlin showed behind his bait. I yelled at him. He didn't hear. The marlin hit. I yelled louder.

"What?" he faintly called.

A marlin is a fighting fish

"Come and grab your rod, man! A white has just struck!"

Belatedly, he made a rush up the ladder. But he had not had quite time enough to finish his shift. As he charged down the deck, his inadequately secured shorts dropped around his ankles and threw him on his face. Before he could regain his feet and get his breeches organized, the marlin had rejected his bait and swung over behind mine.

There is an etiquette about these matters: whoever hooks the fish must catch him or the fish is not "fair caught." I set my reel on free-spool and tried to hand my rod to my friend, but he was still pants-bound. So I struck and I took the marlin—a seventy-two-pounder, on nine-thread. I think I proved my point about excitement in the subsequent fight with the fish. But my editor friend has always felt somewhat gypped in the matter: it was his marlin until he decided to quit fishing and get those shorts.

Another pal and I once used a white marlin to play a trick upon a mutual friend—a visiting fireman from Los Angeles. This gentleman, six feet three and about 220 pounds, an ex-football player, given to calling us "shrimps," went fishing with us one day and hooked the white. We could see on the first leap that the fish ran in the fifty- to sixty-pound class. A little one. After about the tenth leap and the fifth run, we could also see that our 220-pound associate was getting bushed. So we began to tease him gently.

The course of the contest, for some reason known only to the marlin, had meanwhile taken us inshore so that the boat now idled around over a sandy bottom some fifty or sixty feet below. And at that point the despairing marlin gave a last rush away and a frantic leap—in which he managed to throw a half hitch of leader wire around his tail. It pulled up tight, with the fish still slightly curved, so that the fish became a bow and the leader the bowstring. This not entirely rare event paralyzes the fish. He can no longer swim and immediately settles toward bottom, soon to be drowned by the pumping of the angler.

So it happened.

The white marlin sank and sank and drowned and hit bottom and the forward drifting of the boat pulled out a little line as the fish dragged through the sand. Our inexperienced angler, believing this to be a sign of further fight and unaware of the real situation, went wearily and desperately to work again. This gave me an idea. Remembering how often I had been called a shrimp by the gent (I'm 5 10½ and weigh 165) and how often he had called fishing a sissy sport, I had the skipper gun the boat ahead for about three hundred yards. The dead marlin, dragging in the sand, took out at least half that much line. In agony, the gentleman from L. A. worked it back. The skipper gunned again on my signal and the tormented ex-footballer had it to do all over. This system was continued ad lib for the best part of another hour—making a modest-sized dead marlin do the work of a larger, live one, until my pal and I decided that the Angelino had taken all he could safely stand. We then let him bring the leader-bound, deceased fish to boat.

He spent the next three days in bed with exhaustion, prostration, charley horses, massage, infrared lamps and so on. He regards the capture of his fifty-five-pound marlin as the sports achievement of his days. It adorns his office, mounted in full panoply, and unless he reads these lines he will never know that he got a blue-marlin workout from that little white.

It is the quest of the big blue marlin, however, that taxes the patience of all fishermen and drives them to apogees of effort. Think, for instance, of going to the best fishing grounds in the best part of the marlin season, starting out every morning at seven or eight, trolling all day and until sunset without a strike of any kind, starting again the next day—on the hot, blue summer sea off Bimini, and the next, and the next, and so on—without seeing a fish or getting a single strike for *twenty-two consecutive days!*

I did that once. For twenty-two straight days I sat by myself in the cockpit, with two baits out, and fished all day—while the crew stayed up topside in the breeze under a sun-shade. I was alone the whole time. I got to know myself pretty well. But I didn't get a fish. And on the twenty-third day I had to go back home to Miami. That, of course, was the day the blues came in.

Such ardors explain the many sorts of odd behavior that occur when a marlin is found, hooked, and approaches capture.

They explain, for example, the act of a mate who watched a customer fight a four-hundred-pound blue to a standstill, grabbed the leader, and led the exhausted fish to the boatside—only to have the hook pull out. There—inches from capture, was the great prize, slowly sinking in the blue Gulf Stream—inert, licked, all but dead. The mate couldn't stand it. He dived into the sea, grabbed the giant by the bill, swam furiously until

73

he surfaced, and caught a rope. Mate and marlin both were boated!

These excitements also explain why a Mr. A hasn't any right thumb. As he brought his first blue marlin to boat, the mate, heaving in the long leader wire, accidentally threw a loop of it around Mr. A's neck. He was still seated in the fighting chair, at his rod, as is proper. At the moment the loop of wire went over his head, the marlin broke loose from the mate's grasp. Mr. A, not wanting to be beheaded by the drawn-up loop (which he would have been), thrust his thumb under the wire and lifted it up over his head. He did not have time, however, to free his thumb, so the wire came tight on it and cut it off. All hands on board swear to what happened next.

The fish was still hooked. Mr. A adjusted his reel and braced himself against the run. He whipped out a clean handkerchief, took the weight of the fish on his shoulders, then tightly wrapped his bleeding wound. He next reached down, picked his thumb from the deck, calmly dropped it in a pocket, and proceeded to bring back the marlin to the boatside. When it had been heaved aboard—and only then—he gave his injury a more effective dressing while he headed for shore and a doctor.

Blue-marlin fishing is expensive. But four men, dividing the charter of a boat, can fish for blues as reasonably as they can indulge in any of a dozen other sports.

Let any skeptic try it—if, that is, his doctor tells him he's in reasonable condition—and if he's the sort of chap who doesn't lack patience or care what happens when all hell breaks loose. For if he does get his blue, he'll find that he sits around quite smugly afterward as colleagues boast about the touchdown they made for dear old Yale, or the time they took a first in the high hurdles, or the tiger they bagged in India.

When all such as these get done with brag, he can begin.

"Ever catch a blue marlin?"

It's always a peach of a story.

Marine middleweights

Few anglers have ever hung a sea lion. I am one of the few. It happened off the coast of Southern California. We were trolling near a rocky sea-lion-swarming shore and I hung a yellowtail. One of the mammals that had been disporting hard by charged my fish under water. The first warning I had of his presence was a redoubled tug on my line. The second evidence was the sea lion's face, breaking water, right behind my fish. The animal bit my fish in two, even as my boat companions yelled and waved clubs at it—a disturbance ignored by the beast, which presently snatched the inert half of my quarry—and got the hook. His ensuing (and probably horrified) "run" was long, fast and in every way remarkable. All my line was ripped out. It broke. The entire "action" took, I'd guess, about half the time required to read this paragraph.

However, from the power and velocity exhibited by the mammal, I would judge that very few anglers indeed have ever "fought" a hooked sea lion for much longer. None has been "boated" by that method. A sea lion, I would say—from other and equally startling experiences—has about as much malarky as a big porpoise. I have, owing to similar accidents of thieving, hooked porpoises while aiming at kingfish. Nobody has ever caught a porpoise on a light rod, either—or any rod, so far as I have been able to learn. In fact, I regard fishing for porpoises and sea lions as a low trick, like poisoning bears, since they have brains and are conscious and are like dogs rather than fishes.

But such adventures have set me thinking of excitement connected with kingfish, yellowtail and the like, the "middleweights" of the sea. Going after them is not usually regarded as a primary sport amongst deep-sea anglers (a few species are to be excepted, as I shall show) although the middleweights offer thrills uncountable and require great skill. Unfortunately, they are too frequently hooked by people trolling for bigger game and using, in consequence, tackle too large for this class. Furthermore, some people scorn them, especially the inshore or coastal breeds. One of the first deep-sea guides with whom I fished, the late Captain George Fizzell, used to refer to 'cudas, jacks, groupers and the like as "reef trash."

His day was ruined whenever his customers insisted on trolling "inside" the Gulf Stream.

But Gulf Stream fishing, like all blue-water, big-fish angling, can be slow. I have recorded in these very pages how once I trolled for twenty-two consecutive days from dawn to dark for blue marlin—without getting a strike of any kind. Of course, I was using big baits—whole bonefish of between three and seven pounds each—and smaller baits might easily have attracted other, if lesser, fishes. But twenty-two days of strikeless trolling is a long time and costs a lot of money; I felt as a wildcat oilman must when he finally concedes the hole he has drilled is dry. People who go sailfishing are aware of the comparative scarcity, at times, of that gamester. They often ask, "If the sails aren't hitting, is there a chance of anything else?" There always is: the middleweights.

What do I mean by the term? I mean that galaxy of ocean species which normally weigh between five and fifty pounds, fish as game—relatively—as the prized marlin, broadbill, mako shark, bluefin and yellowfin tuna, sailfish, and so on. Fish of such sorts abound in many waters if not most. Some, such as the "school tuna," furnish a separate division of angling sport. But off Florida, California, the Bahamas, islands of the Pacific and the Mediterranean coast (to mention just a few locales) the medium-sized fishes of the reef are responsible for the bulk of the sportsman's catch—as well as for sundry cults and local enthusiasms. The angler trolling in deeper water, say for white marlin or sailfish, may well come in without either—and yet feel satisfied with a catch of dolphin, bonito, barracuda, albacore and perhaps, on a lucky day, a big wahoo. None of these fish is likely to weigh more than fifty pounds—though most of them might. Every one is a double handful of blister-raising fish power.

For example, I have always maintained that a little-known fish called arctic bonito, which seldom weighs more than fifteen pounds, is, for his size, the strongest fish that swims. Admittedly, that opinion is open to question—even to argument—and if staunchly held it can lead to fist-fighting. However, this bonito takes baits of a size intended for sailfish, as well as feathers and spoons. His fighting is done under water—he seldom breaks the surface until you pull him out. But if you hang an arctic bonito on such gear as you would normally use for largemouth bass, muskellunge or salmon, you will be given a thought-provoking experience: you won't catch the bonito; you will merely lose your line. The sheer speed, power and doggedness of this cobalt-and-silver-streaked powerhouse will dumfound you. On sailfish gear, of course, it's a different story—but who would hunt quail with cannon and shrapnel? Most arctic bonito, sadly enough, are taken by people trolling for sails with heavy tackle.

The dolphin, more numerous, more widely distributed, is more celebrated. He is stronger for his weight than the sailfish. He (or she—for among dolphins the sexes are readily told apart) is also a leaping fish. Sails and marlins could learn much about aerial gymnastics from dolphin. This blue-spotted, green, gold and azure creature, moreover, is handsomer than any trout: dolphins are so beautiful that Shelley wrote a poem about them. They are so stunning to watch, in a clear sea, with the sun shining on them, that I've repeatedly seen anglers lose them because, once they sighted the dolphins, their eyes popped, their jaws dropped and they forgot to go on fishing. They just stared and exclaimed. One man, even, to get a better look, put down his rod and leaned far over the gunwale. He lost the rod and the fish, too—and we nearly lost him before he gave up gazing! That time (as often), when one fish had been hooked, a whole school came up to see what was going on —an incandescent green, gold and blue-dappled horde as radiant as a swarm of two-foot butterflies.

There is, while the subject of beauty is under discussion, a beautiful grouper. Generally, the grouper (a kind of sea bass) is regarded as ugly. He has an outsize mouth—which yawns open and makes a formidable brake in the last stages of a battle with him. He is brownish and blackish and mottled like a toad. But a grouper called rock hind, though he has considerable color variation, specializes in brilliant reds and is spotted from mouth to tail with deep scarlet or crimson. The yellow-fin grouper is on the pretty side, also; and it should be noted that even the most dazzling grouper is as delicious in chowder as the most drab—which says much, since grouper chowder is good enough to make a Yankee forget about clams.

Groupers are inshore or "reef" fish, although out on the deeper bottom lives one—the warsaw grouper—whose weight may exceed four hundred pounds. We used to fish for them, using a breakaway lead of some twenty pounds on a cable so rigged that once the fish was hung, the weight could be winched back to the boat. These big fish, however, aren't fighters. As you heave them surfaceward, the pressure diminishes and the air inside them expands so that the fish swells grotesquely, dies—even bursts! On the other hand, we've found certain snappers of fifteen to twenty pounds which, if brought up swiftly from even as much as six hundred feet, hardly swell at all and arrive very much alive. Why the difference, none can say as yet. Scientists are studying the subject.

The grouper is my favorite ocean fish to eat. He is easy to catch, will hit almost any kind of bait (including a rag, by test!) and is regarded as only mildly game. This is owing to the fact that he is usually taken on too-heavy tackle. On light tackle, a grouper can be a piscatorial problem for anybody. Part of the reason is his usual custom, when hooked, of trying to bore back down and among the corals where he lives. Corals are exceedingly sharp and a fish plunging amongst hills of them—among arcades, tunnels, natural bridges, shelves and other formations—usually cuts the line. Perhaps if he doesn't manage that, he does contrive to get into a spot where he can brace himself and hang on. Then the angler gives him slack, even as with a small pond fish caught amongst snags, and waits in the hope the grouper will tire of playing 'possum and emerge. I've seen an angler wait an hour for that to happen—*and win.*

But another reason for taking interest in groupers is this: sometimes they don't merely bore down toward bottom till spent. I've seen groupers leap more than once and I've even, on one occasion, seen a grouper *greyhound* after a trolling bait, just like a dolphin—or a marlin! Moreover, groupers are strong. Off Turtle Rock, near Bimini, some years ago, while fishing with Captain Eddie Wall on the *Playmate,* I saw a grouper—a fifty- or sixty-pounder, charge an amberjack. I'd been fighting on light tackle for half an hour. The *Playmate* was lying dead in the water, the sea was glassy calm, the sun was directly overhead and my amberjack was on the small side—about thirty pounds. The grouper hit him, shook him, and in an instant bit (or broke) him in two, rushing off with the larger half. Many old-time anglers have doubted that tale; but I saw it happen and so did the guides.

Groupers, also, when the notion occurs to them, will fight right on the surface—making long runs which supply in power what they lack (when compared with the runs, say, of a wahoo) in speed. They may even fight with their dorsal fin out, like a shark. And sharks may be the reason for this occasional, atypical style of battle: Sometimes a hooked grouper may prefer the surface to his usual downward dive, owing to the fact that he knows, somewhere below, a shark is waiting and watching interestedly. At least, that's the only reasonable explanation we've ever hit upon for the surface-fighting grouper.

The all-time down-boring champion, however, is the amberjack, and his Pacific relative, the yellowtail. An amberjack is definitely a reef fish although sometimes caught in blue water. Amongst the middleweights his working style may be compared with that of the mule or burrow. Catch him and you will see he is all "shoulder." He gets big—up to and a bit over a hundred pounds. Blunt-nosed, amber and silver with vague purplish marks and iridescences, the amberjack hits anything, though he prefers live fish. He often travels in schools and lives in families so that he shares with the dolphins a frequent custom of inspecting *en famille* a hooked fellow fish. This means that, when you have finally whipped down one big amberjack and brought him in toward your boat for gaffing, he may be accompanied by a half-dozen—*or a hundred!*—companions. This, in turn, means that while your captain is gaffing, the mate may be baiting up another rod.

Hence, just as your fish is boated and you wearily open a beer or light a cigarette to rest, the mate hands you a new rod, and steps to the stern. He peers down into the water, picks the largest amberjack he can spot in the tarrying school and tries to toss the live bait—perhaps a half- or one-pound grunt or yellowtail (in this case, not the Pacific fish but a small, Atlantic species—no relation) right into grandpa amberjack's jaws. Sometimes the mate does it. I've done it myself. Sometimes the tossed-in bait becomes the center of an amberjack merry-go-round staged in three dimensions and as many directions as meridians take; but somebody nearly always gets the bait before it's stripped from the hook. The gimmick is, being the angler, being tired, you're nevertheless once again hooked to something like a wrong-way V_2—one, that is, headed not for the stratosphere but the infernal regions.

And this sequential fishing can go on and on and on. Just how long, nobody knows. Few living men have taken six amberjack of large size in a row, fewer still have caught ten in a series. So few, at any rate, that I've never read or heard of it or seen it happen—though I've seen when it *could* have happened. For I recall one pleasant season in Bimini when one of the world's greatest anglers and I (one of the world's most fluent discoursers on deep-sea angling) were nettled, not to say indignant, that some guests came aboard armed to and above the teeth, maybe cowlick high, with bowie knives, sharp machetes, killing spears, lances and assorted guns of the elephant and buckshot kind. These gents—well enough educated to know better—were loaded for—what? Hostile spaceship inhabitants, it looked like.

My friend and I earnestly sought trouble for these two gents—but trouble was hard to find far at sea that day. The water was poured-metal calm. Marine fish often knock off hitting surface baits under such conditions. Possibly they think kills would be too easy. Anyhow, strikeless, we moved in over the reef. There below us, for four hours, paraded neck and neck, feet apart, a march of amberjack about two hundred yards wide and we don't know how long. Miles, many miles—they were still parading, much like migrating tuna, but without major breaks in ranks and without "schooling," when darkness fell. We tossed live baits into this transient horde of what seemed like all the amberjack in the world.

Fish were hooked; battles started; and each hooked fish was accompanied, during the fight, by from six to a dozen companions. Often these accompanying fish snatched bits of the trailing bait right from the jaws of their hooked associates. Indeed, if we'd had the rigs (and the muscle, and the nonsporting desire), we could undoubtedly have hooked three or four or five of these fish at a time, on one setup. This "show" was plainly visible to all of us except the anglers because of the clarity and calmness of the sea; the anglers themselves missed it—they were too busy angling. The moment one or other of them boated or lost a fish, one of us stood by with a new rod, reel, line and baited hook ready. For, as soon as the other angler got his fish near the boat, the "escort" was within tossing range. We would pick out the biggest fish and throw a bait directly at him. The eye would roll, the big jaws snap, and the angler's contest would start anew.

Our armed-to-the-teeth guests caught four or five amberjack apiece before they gave up, exhausted. Toward the end, they had such weary arms and shoulders they were using their *knees* to help pump the rods. These amberjack ran from forty to seventy pounds. It made for a nice day, and in the days that followed the knife-toting gentlemen stopped going down to the sea with their arsenals. In fact, for one whole day, they didn't fish at all; they stayed in bed; somehow, their muscles wouldn't work.

The wahoo, a member of the mackerel family, a fish with a silly name, is one whose silliness ends right there. Striped like a tiger in light and dark blues that fade as he dies, and given a tiger's bounding speed, the wahoo has sharp teeth, power, hits anything that trolls if he's in the mood, and can be found— though rarely, in most waters—almost any place that's offshore and tropical or subtropical. For a racy, surface fight, he is recommended strongly. Behind my desk is a picture of my daughter and beside her in the picture is a wahoo notably taller, as it hangs from the rack, than she is. Karen is five feet, three and a half. The wahoo's near six feet. It weighed seventy-odd pounds and it took Karen, who is experienced in such matters, more than half an hour on *marlin tackle* to get her wahoo connected with a gaff. Never, as they say in Philadelphia, underestimate the power of a woman. Or a wahoo.

During the Second World War our Government sent to its troops the world over pocket-sized editions of myriads of books by American authors. Among the titles were three collections of fishing tales written by this scribe. As a result, I received thousands of letters from young Americans who were fishing in all sorts of waters. Some fished because they were hungry for meat. Of these, some fished not with hooks and lines but hand grenades and materials intended for demolition. One lad, however, sent me some snapshots of an enormous wahoo caught in the remote Pacific. And this sailor, whose accompanying letter insisted that wahoo of more than two hundred pounds had been lost by him, owing to the lightness of available gear, convinced me. In my files I have his map of reefs, off a certain island, inhabited by the giant wahoo and I am carefully keeping the document against the day when it's barely possible I might find my way to the area. A two-hundred-pound wahoo would be worth traveling toward!

Of course, a two-hundred-pound fish can hardly be called a "middleweight." But that's another enchantment of this classification of fishes. In the reaches of the seven seas, the size of fish of one species will vary. You may be hunting for a kind of which a giant would weigh fifty pounds—only to hit into a super-giant (astronomical terms being not inappropriate here) touching a hundred. And most fish have relatives, close cousins, that run bigger than they do. There's that warsaw grouper we catch by special means off Miami, for instance, that can weigh four hundred pounds or more. I've even heard tell, for instance, of five-hundred-pound sailfish in the Indian Ocean, someplace—though there's nearly always a big jump between what you hear told—and what the scales finally say.

Here, there or elsewhere, probably twenty sorts of fish are called "kingfish." One king, the king mackerel, is widely sought off Florida. A game, but not savage, fish, the "king" of Florida waters travels as a rule in schools, immense schools —he is fished commercially as well as for sport. Many so-called sportsmen, however, fish for kings less for fine angling than for quantity—using feathers or spoons, heavy sinkers, and a heavy-wire trolling line. Such gear, by taking the bait down deep, admittedly attracts far more kings than do surface baits —and kings are worth catching just to eat. Whoever denies this either doesn't like fish or doesn't know how to cook. Such gear, however, destroys the combat as a sport and kingfish, even on fairly light tackle, are modest fighters. As if to make up for that, however, they do have one trick so fantastic that it must be seen to be appreciated.

I'll never forget my first sight of the spectacle. We were trolling down along the Florida Keys towards Islamorada, years back. Something—something silver and white and biggish—came out of the sea and started climbing like a jet plane. Afterward, I insisted it went as high as the outriggers—and they were about twenty-five feet tall. Perhaps it only went twenty feet up. Anyhow, the sky was that blue blaze of light familiar in the region and the thing flew up so fast I was sure, for a split second, it was some sort of *bird* that had been under water until our boat passed by. However, the upward curve became a parabola and what I then perceived to be a fish came down, with incredible accuracy considering the jump, *squarely on the bait*. "King," the skipper murmured, as the fish vanished beneath the surface, the outrigger line fell, and I tried to change shock into sensible, fast action. Kings can do that—the king mackerel of the region—and I would bet on them even against tarpon in a seagoing track meet, as high jumpers. And kings can do it the other way around, as I was to see for myself, years later, off Miami. They can come up directly *under* a trolled surface bait, grab it on the rise, and *then* soar into the sky in a breath-taking leap, carrying line and bait in their jaws and actually hooking themselves in lofty mid-air!

In the middleweight classification, too, go all the jacks besides amberjack. Crevallé jack, horse-eye jack, almaco jack and many more. These are cousins of the pompano, and a couple of pompano should be on the list also: the African, which has streaming dorsal fins—no one knows why—and the permit, a pompano about whom somebody should write a book.

The jack is not a leaping fish, as can be noted from the description already given of the amberjack in action. But he and all his relatives are fast and busy. How fast? Here is the perennial angling question. This much I can say. Jacks live well when impounded in salt-water ponds made by fencing in a bit of ocean with wire, rocks or whatnot. Years back, in Key West, there used to be such a pond, inhabited by jacks, barracuda, groupers and the like. These fish were reasonably "tame" and, at mealtime, would come up in mixed schools to the shore, waiting for food. The food consisted of hunks of cut-up fish and a chunk the size of a table-tennis ball would be pitched with great velocity. It was perhaps fifty feet across the pond and the jacks, seeing a man bracing himself to throw, would turn about and face out, like runners waiting for a starting gun. I have seen baseball players throw chunks of meat as hard as they could across that pond. But I have never seen the meat hit the water when there wasn't a jack underneath, waiting—a crevallé jack that had covered the same distance a bit faster than the man could throw. How fast this is, in the case of a chunk of meat, I don't know. But mighty fast—especially when you consider the fish had a standing start, and was obliged, furthermore, to take note of the direction of the throw by looking up through a foot or more of water at a small object zooming through the air. Thirty miles an hour would be very conservative.

This kind of speed, attached to rod and reel, in the person of a fish weighing ten or twenty pounds or less or even more, provides extremely interesting combat. Jacks, like groupers, are very wise in using rough coral architecture and snags, such as fallen logs, to discomfit anglers. They are also abundant, in wide areas. Crevallés and horse-eyes inhabit inshore areas as a rule and may be taken from beaches, rowboats, docks, or by wading on the flats. They will hit top-water plugs so hard that only rugged ones last long—the others fall apart. They can be taken on ordinary casting tackle. But the man who goes after them without a thumbstall (or a few layers of adhesive wound round his thumb) will be in trouble. Thus, the initial run of an eight-pound horse-eye jack I took in Bimini the first day I tried for them gave me such a bad turn that I couldn't use that thumb for a couple of weeks.

However—and here's an invaluable tip for bait casters who are salt-water tyros—if you haven't a thumbstall and your casting reel begins to heat up your thumb, the thing to do to save yourself a blister is to plunge rod, reel, hand and all into the water. This provides automatic, instant cooling. Besides, the reel handles, whizzing in the sea, are slowed down—an effect which provides considerable drag and lets you ease up with the overheated thumb. This I learned while tarpon fishing with a casting outfit—after I'd had the somber experience with horse-eyes.

Amberjack usually hang around coral reefs where the water's from twenty to upward of a hundred feet deep. Crevallés and horse-eyes are inshore jacks. The permit, a relative, is also a shallow-water denizen. A flattish, wide fish with a bluish dorsal fin like a scimitar, a fish that feeds like a bonefish—i.e., by nosing along in a dozen inches of salt water, hunting for crabs and the like, with his dorsal or tail often showing—the permit runs up to at least forty pounds. There are plenty of anglers who will swear he is the fastest, toughest thing in fins, pound for pound and, as I hinted, he's worth going after. In some areas permit are fairly abundant. They are generally taken by using bait—crabs and such—presented by a cast after stalking (for a feeding permit can be seen a long way off). The cast is followed by a breathless wait while the blue dorsal and paddling tail approach the spot where the bait lies.

The African pompano—a permit and jack relation—is usually caught over fairly deep reefs and sometimes in the edge of the Gulf Stream—on baits being trolled for sailfish and the like. He is a hard-fighting fish that has, like the permit, a curious habit of turning on his side in the water to get the utmost out of himself. And this pompano is artistically dramatic. His

91

dorsal fin is elongated in "streamers," a half dozen of which may trail a couple of feet behind. Nobody knows for sure their function. But a good guess would be this: Even though you might be a thirty-pound fish, you would find the ocean a perilous place to live with far bigger fishes forever trying to sneak up from the rear and make a meal of you; if, however, you were trailing streamers behind you, they might act as a warning-device; any huge fish, stretching his jaws and closing in to devour you, would first touch the streamers—at which point, without bothering to look around, you could open the throttle to full speed and take evasive action. I suspect the African pompano is one of the few fish to be provided with rear-end antennae.

The almaco is a deepwater jack, caught rather rarely. There are many other pompano relatives and jacks taken the world around. One such, for instance, gave me what might have been my one good chance at immortality. I was reef fishing along the picturesque islets north of Cat Cay one morning when I hung what I deemed to be a small jack, as indeed it was—an eight-to-ten-pounder. When I boated it, however, I noted at once that it was not like any jack known to me. It was fatter, chubbier, or stubbier. Besides which, it was violet —all over. A very beautiful thing to see. The skipper, mate and native boys on board had never in their fishful lives seen one before. We put it tenderly on ice. We went in for lunch. After lunch, I went to the icebox to prepare the specimen for a fast air trip to Miami where Al Pfleuger, the famed taxidermist, would identify it if that could be done, and, if not, mount it and preserve the skeleton. Unfortunately, while I had my lunch, some island boys, searching for a lunch for themselves, found the fish, filleted it, threw the carcass overboard, fried the meat and ate it. Inasmuch as I have never since heard of a purple or violet-colored jack, I possibly missed having my name preserved forever in some such Latin form as *Pompano indigoiensis Wylieae.*

That's the thing about sea fishing. You never know. You may be "after" a special kind of fish with the bait and angling method designed for it, specifically—and catch twelve other kinds but never the one you were seeking. Or you may be trying to get a fish of a certain size, approximately, and hang its grandfather instead. That happens with monotonous frequency in the case of tarpon. Several outdoor magazines have published full reports of tarpon—and since they run way over two hundred pounds they are not exactly "middleweights." But men with bait-casting rods—and fly-casting rods, too!—search out regions where the tarpon are in scale. In my opinion, fishing provides nothing closer to four-alarm fires than the uproar afforded by ten or thirty or fifty pounds of tarpon in one piece, attached to light tackle. However, the man who flings out plugs in the hope of hooking such tarpon can—and often does—experience the calamity of having his bait taken by a tarpon pushing a couple of hundred pounds. With a mere hundred yards of twelve-pound test line, the bird in that predicament can only sit, while his thumb heats (and perhaps the tarpon's leaps drench him with buckets of water), until the fish meanders off, breaking the line.

93

Some fish

Readers will note my mention of barracuda—certainly a Grade A game fish for the middleweight division. 'Cudas leap, bulldog, sound, make fast surface runs and generally behave—on light tackle—like a poor man's marlin. But you will remember I reported on the breed fully in an earlier chapter. Suffice to say here that 'cudas are fascinating to fish for, good to eat, and may be found in tropical and semitropical waters anywhere and everywhere—lying close inshore like pike (which are distant relatives), or roaming the great Gulf Stream where bottom lies five hundred fathoms down.

Some small sharks should be classified as middleweights, also—particularly little black-tips—often taken on light gear in such vast regions as the Bay of Florida. But, again, I have previously expounded on sharks in these pages.

Besides the fishes I have already mentioned as middleweights, there are *hundreds* more. Literally. There is, for example, the so-called "school tuna"—a fish running (generally) from twenty-five pounds up to seventy-five—which is the object of summer-pursuit by fleets of charterboats in New Jersey, on Long Island, and elsewhere. This tuna is neither more nor less than a young bluefin—the childhood form of the giant "horse mackerel," a physically perfect chip off the old block, with the same power, stubbornness, tendency to sound, and excess of energy.

The first really definite impression I made on the girl who is now my wife was achieved by means of the school tuna. She and a friend and I were spending a day at the sport when the friend and I hung a double-header—his first school tuna, incidentally. We got them to the boat at the same time, after a half hour of walloping battle. His was gaffed—mine got away. I was delighted that he'd caught one—and not in the least miffed by missing, since I'd taken hundreds and lost even more. The lady who is now Mrs. Wylie, however, mistook my mixture of enthusiasm and nonchalance for extreme sportsmanship and, as she later confessed, admired it greatly! The gent who caught the fish has never before or since registered a more abundant, whooping form of delight—even though he's very good at registering emotion, being Paul Douglas, then a radio announcer and now a star of the stage and the movies.

In Florida waters we have a cousin of this tuna, an albacore, a fish usually running around the ten-to-fifteen-pound mark, prized for his battling heart and even more for his flavor —when boiled and cooled—in salad. In the Pacific there are yet other albacores, as edible, as given to fighting. Moreover, what I would call an albacore, in certain areas, is called a bonito.

There is a fish called the snook, too. Snooks like shallow water, hollows under stumps, weed-thick coves, and other such places as pike inhabit. Snooks, indeed, with barracudas, are distant relatives of the pike-pickerel-muskie tribe. I like to use the snook to help a fresh-water angler, a fly caster or bait caster, make the transition to ocean fishing. His gear will be familiar to him. He will not find a great difference between casting his plug at the water alongside a fallen pine tree or the open water amongst lily pads and casting up to a tangle of mangrove roots or into a blue pothole surrounded by shallow water in which red seaweed grows. The snook will hit like a pike and fight like one—with special emphasis on a genius for fouling up the line on snags.

Where snook are scarce, there may be redfish. These are also called red drum, drum, channel bass, and sixteen other names. As fighters they are mediocre, but since they reach well over twenty pounds, their weight adds problems of an interesting nature to, say, the fly-fisherman. Like bonefish and permit, they may be spotted from afar, feeding along shoal waters—and stalked. They can be "flushed" or scared away—like bonefish and permit, too—but not so easily. A flushed redfish, for instance, will often start feeding again soon, quite near, and may be stalked anew. It is quite interesting, not to say palsy-making, to fish the way you often hunt—spotting the game first, taking dead aim, bulleting out a plug, and then—just where the fun of hunting ends, to have the biggest fun of fishing still in store!

It isn't possible to make this sportsman's log all-inclusive: There aren't pages enough to contain the full log of the middleweights. What has preceded is a mere sampling, a kind of *indication* of fishes which fall in this fabulous class. I haven't mentioned the other drums, the celebrated striped bass (about which books *have* been written), or a fish that baffles and excites anglers from Cuba to Chesapeake Bay—the crabeater, or cobia. Honorable mention certainly should go to the mackerels —Spanish and cero. Several of the snappers would qualify— indeed, I've seen one that had weighed more than a hundred pounds—stuffed and hanging in the old Key Largo Club, where it was proudly placed by the man who took it, the late Tom Frasure, a Florida guide who had his greatest pleasure angling for the middleweights and who was a demon snapper-catcher.

Roosterfish should be on the list—and hogfish. Perhaps blackfish qualify. The smaller, inshore members of the jewfish family belong here, though their sires and dams, running to many hundred of pounds, rate a different listing. Some anglers would add devilfish, by which I mean squid, taken occasionally off Chile on rod and reel by angler-pioneers who don't mind wild seas, night fishing, tentacles wrapping around their necks, ink squirted in their faces and the hideous spectacle of mass cannibalism in the rough, luminous water. But this will suffice, I trust, to convince the angler who, up to now, has felt marine fishing is a matter of long days of trolling which may or may not wind up with a monster caught, that such is not the case necessarily. With sailfish baits flickering from out-riggers and lines trolling straight back, with a cruiser or even an outboard guided in broad scallops around the Gulf Stream edge, you may, to be sure, raise sails. But you may, instead, raise and hang a dozen other sorts of fish—and when the day ends, you may well have forgotten that, all the while, it was sailfish you were seeking, not kings and mackerel, 'cudas, groupers, amberjack, dolphin, bonito, wahoos, and the like. You will go back again for sails, of course; but you won't count that day lost, believe me.

It was, in fact, the lowly kingfish which started me on a twenty-five-year ocean-fishing cruise. Way back then, I'd gone to Miami for my health. I was a trout fisherman in those days, a black-bass expert of sorts, an old pickerel, pike, dory and muskellunge angler, a fresh-water man. I chartered a boat, and all we caught was kings that day. But no one can imagine my state of mind. They were as big as muskies. They fought hard. And in that single day, I caught more than thirty! The very next week, I started for the Keys in a charterboat—and not that year and not the next did I take a sailfish, let alone a marlin. Just various members of the middleweight division.

They led—at long last—and this is a general rule—to sails, marlin, tuna and the like. But let me put it this way. If I had never caught anything bigger, I'd still be out there hunting the ones in the middle. For there isn't *actually* a dependable "middle." A month or so ago I went down to the docks in Bimini to see the head of a dolphin. The island was babbling about it. And there it lay—just the head—chopped off less than a foot behind the eyes by some sea giant. But what a head! It weighed more than thirty pounds! Neptune alone knows how long, how heavy, that giant old bull dolphin must have been! The part of his dorsal left intact was eight inches tall. We estimated—and "we" includes some mighty conservative scientists at the Marine Laboratory on Bimini—that he would have run *well over a hundred pounds*. A dolphin, that is— a "middleweight" fish—which might possibly have surpassed the world-record weight of the Atlantic sailfish! In the sea, then, no matter what you think you're fishing *for*—you never *know*.

That gigantic dolphin had smashed at a blue marlin bait. But, then, innocent people trolling for groupers have hung five-hundred-pound marlin! Which is why a last word of warning is necessary, when fishing for the middle-sized denizens of the deep is under discussion. *Be ready to hang what you're seeking—or just about anything else!* Exploring the kingdom of middle-sized ocean fishes is much like lighting a fuse without being exactly sure of the size or nature of the explosive charge on the other end. Fun—but *brother*—watch it!

Some fishermen and
fishing spots

Miami invites you to fish

Among the highest of high spots possible to a great many men—ladies too!—is one which occurs when the fresh-water fisherman first casts a fly, or a plug, or trolls a spoon, or drops a bait, in tropical salt water. All anglers are hereby invited, if in Miami, to take a fling at what might well turn out to be one of their greatest adventures. This invitation is also extended to that benighted group of persons who never fished—for, in Miami, anything can happen to anybody. I saw one gent, who had never wet a fish line in his life, come in from half a day on the Gulf Stream with the only broadbill swordfish taken that year! It weighed more than two hundred and fifty pounds!

What is said in the discussion that follows will be addressed to salt-water novices. There are two reasons for this. Men who have already fished in the sea and who propose to visit Miami sometime will undoubtedly plan a spell of angling —and they will know what kind they want to try. But those who have not fished there at all, unaware of the true circumstances, and lacking suitable information, may miss the kind of fishing they would most enjoy. In some cases, the legends of the prowess required for salt-water angling may scare them off altogether. That would be an unmitigated disaster. For, while it is entirely true that certain anglers get themselves into peak condition so as to be able to struggle for hours with various marine giants, it is equally true that barefoot boys go down to the sea with cane poles and come home with eye-popping strings of this and that.

So, at the outset, one common, false impression must be corrected. Any kind of fresh-water fishing that you have enjoyed has a salt-water parallel. Note that I do not say "equivalent"; later on, you will see why. Let us suppose that you are a shore fisherman. You like to sit with a long pole or a hand line, on which is a sinker and a hook and some bait. In this fashion, you have taken bullheads, rock bass, sunnies, an occasional black bass, and the like. You need no different tackle —and only such a different bait as shrimp—to catch not one kind of fish but any of *hundreds* of sorts, from banks, the sides of brackish canals, bridges, beaches, and other points where land meets water.

Among these may well be grunts and porgies and snappers—which may be compared with sunnies and perch, though they may run up to so many pounds in weight as to astonish you, and break your line! Among these may also be salt-water catfish, trout, jacks, grouper, and the whole gaudy repertoire (especially if you use very small hooks) of "tropical" fish—the angelfishes, butterfly fish, triggers, parrots, and so on.

That begins to give you an idea. And summertime, contrary to the fears of some, is the *best* time for fishing in south Florida. There isn't any season, actually. "It's always," as the slogan says, "June in Miami"—well, nearly always. And the fish are hungry year round. People who have assumed that Miami's "fishing season" is winter have done so merely because that is when the tourists abound most thickly in the area—i.e., when the largest number of people go fishing and when the biggest tournament is held. Actually, we residents concentrate on summer fishing, spring fishing, and autumn fishing because the wintertime angling seems slow by comparison.

I have, of course, put the cart before the horse and mentioned the humblest kind of fishing first, rather than the most elegant. It was done deliberately, to encourage the timid. Before discussing loftier and fancier methods, I wanted the reader to appreciate that, with tackle picked up in a dime store and carried in his pocket, bait bought at a butcher shop, and a couple of hours to spare, he can find plenty of company fishing from any old spot around Miami, and plenty of fish to match luck with.

The classical fishing trip in this area is made by charter-boat for innumerable sorts of quarry, of which the prima donna is the sailfish. Generally speaking, a "charterboat" is a cabin cruiser of from thirty to forty feet with an open cockpit in which are from three to five "fighting chairs"—that is, chairs fixed firmly to the deck and equipped, at the front edge of the seat, with a socket on a gimbal. The angler puts the butt of his rod in the socket, uses one hand to hold the rod and the other for reeling. Charterboats furnish all necessary tackle, bait, and other gear—everything, indeed, except the lunch you will want if you hire one for a whole day, suntan oil (and don't think the sun in Miami isn't a menace without it!) and cameras to snap the expression that will come over your face when you "hang" your first big, sea-going fish.

Charterboats are manned by a captain and a mate who are called "guides." There are several hundred available in the Miami area at numerous fishing docks. You will observe the "fleets" as you barge around the Miamis: they are characterized by their tall "outriggers" and, when docked, present the appearance of a thicket of supersized fishing poles. Most boats are equipped with ship-to-shore radio-telephones so that, if you wish, while you are trolling for big ones, miles offshore, you can call up your office in Chicago and find out what the day's sales were. They are also furnished with comfortable daybeds for napping, with iceboxes for anything you might want to keep on ice, such as marmalade, and they accommodate from one to a maximum of six anglers.

Arrangements for a charterboat may be made through any hotel. Arrangements may be made, also, at any of the fishing docks, with the guides direct. Your hotel will direct you to the nearest of these docks. The cost of a charterboat is considerable—about sixty-five dollars a day—although when this is split five or six ways it will not seem excessive. A "lone wolf," incidentally, will find, by visiting any fishing dock (around five in the afternoon, when the boats come in from fishing, is the best time), that he can arrange to be one of a party on the ensuing day by signing up with any of various boats which have "openings" for one or two additional fishermen.

To pay twelve or fifteen dollars for a day's Gulf-Stream trolling is not, actually, out of line. No charterboatman ever got rich. The initial cost and the upkeep of their elaborate vessels are high. They run all day long—and you would pay far more to ride the same length of time on a passenger train or boat. The guides furnish the tackle and the wear and tear on this expensive gear is prodigious; if you go charterboat fishing and have any kind of a day for it, you will see why that is.

For, off Miami, dwell millions or billions of fishes that have no intention of being taken on anybody's hook and line. The sailfish—a character usually six to eight feet long, with a rapier-like "bill" and a large, indigo dorsal fin with black polka dots, the exact purpose of which is not yet known to any naturalist—runs from thirty pounds up to a world's record of a little more than a hundred. He spends much of his life on the sea-surface, chasing flying, and other, fish. He will chase a bait trolled on the surface and, overtaking it, club it with his bill. If the bait then stops dead in the water and appears to be stunned, the sailfish will generally eat same. Thereafter, depending somewhat on the weight of his tackle, the angler at the other end will have one of the busiest and most enthralling half hours in all his born days. The sail will almost certainly leap from one to umpteen times, trying to shake the hook. He will make runs like a rudderless torpedo. He may come out and "tail-walk"—raging about, boiling up an acre of the sea. He may "sound" and bull around grimly hundreds of feet under water.

The chances of seeing and "hanging" a sailfish in a day's summer trolling are pretty good. The matter of *catching* said sail is something else—a problem always involving luck and, sometimes, skill. Doughty anglers have tried for sails for weeks —and not got one. Mere housewives, frail women in poor condition, who never held a rod before, have caught three of them on their first day out. It's like that.

However, a man trolling for sailfish off Miami in a charter-boat—unlike a man trying for some fresh-water species—say, lake trout—need not come home dispirited if it happens that no sail takes a fancy to his lure. Where the sailfish range, so do the dolphin. Dolphin often go over thirty pounds, sometimes over fifty, and higher. They leap like sailfish and are, in my opinion, the most beautiful of all the big, pelagic fish. And— where the sail and dolphin sport themselves, so do barracuda; these are big marine pike which fight like the renowned mus-kellunge. Here, too, is the home of the bonita and the arctic bonita, the kingfish and the wahoo—and many a charterboat, on single days, gets one of all these, or more.

In going out to the Gulf Stream to troll, boats pass over the great coral reefs which skirt all of southeastern Florida, including the Florida Keys. "Reef fishing" is considered a specialty. On the reef live amberjack and groupers and barracu-das, large snappers and jewfish and other jacks besides the

108

amber guy—shoals and hordes of fish as big as ever you will want to tackle on rod and reel. They are taken in every sort of way—on live bait and cut bait from anchored boats—by trolling (more slowly than for the "outside" fishes) with or without a sinker—by drifting, and so on. But your guide, if he finds the fishing slow in or along the edge of the Gulf Stream, is very likely to cut down the speed of his engines, take you a little closer to shore—over the reefs—and you, the customer, are then likely to find a change of pace in the fishing. Big ones are apt to come up from the weird, coral wonderland fifty or twenty feet under your keel and take hold. Take hold, I ought to say, like a passing mail train.

One more memorandum anent charterboat fishing. Besides the species mentioned, and scores left unmentioned for lack of space, there exist, in the Stream, such fishes as white marlin, Allison tuna, and blue marlin. If you are trolling with ordinary sailfish tackle and a white marlin swats your bait, you have a good chance of getting him—and if you do that, your relatives will grow tired to death, as the years pass, while you keep retelling the tale of that colossal scrap. If a blue marlin or an Allison tuna takes hold—unless your guide has trolled a supersize outfit—your chances of success are trivial. A few hundred yards of line, with a breaking strain of thirty or forty pounds, mean absolutely nothing to a blue marlin of, say, five hundred pounds, who is liable to run a straight, reel-spattering half mile in the first hundred *seconds* after he feels a hook!

I've seen it happen, I suppose, a dozen times: a great, black bill behind a sailfish bait, a smashing strike that throws water twenty feet high, the appalling leap of several hundred pounds of blue-striped blue marine majesty, a run like the take-off of a jet plane—and bing! Broken line. Stripped reel. Or busted rod. But it's worth the price of admission even without the fish. Then, too, I've seen things strike and run and get away that nobody was able to identify—huge, anonymous power-houses of the ocean deep.

If you like milder fishing in landlocked, calmer waters, there are guides with smaller boats who, for half the price of a charterboat, will take you trolling all day in the Bay. And there are several "party" boats—large ships which anchor on the reefs; from the decks of these, scores of anglers, at two or three dollars a head, with their own tackle, fish the day long in any manner they please. Information about Bay fishing (for persons worried over seasickness) or about the "party" boats may be had at the regular charterboat docks, at hotels, and from the Miami Chamber of Commerce. By the same means, fishing trips to Florida's rivers and lakes, where large-mouth bass abound, may be arranged.

All, or nearly all the foregoing, sounds rather foreign to the fresh-water angler. But for him, Miami and the adjacent seas have something very special. Perhaps you hate the sea. Possibly you get sick. (If the latter, you should visit your doctor and have him prescribe the new seasick remedy; it works.) But it may well be that you like to cast a dry fly for trout, or a wet fly, or that you are an old salmon man, or a plug caster who thinks it is a waste of time to fish with anything but a light rod, a level-wind reel, fifteen-pound test line and artificial lures.

During the past two decades, anglers in the Miami area have developed what amounts to a new world of sports fishing

—fishing in salt water by all the above methods. In the bays and on the "flats" off the Keys, in the salt-water canals and off beaches are thousands of fish-filled *square miles* of shallow water. The territory is accessible by car, rowboat, outboard motor, and by a little walking, in some instances. Various parts of it recommend themselves to the brook angler and his fly rod, the plug caster, and so on. A two-hour drive from Miami into the Keys, and a little questioning at any of the countless camps open to the public in the Keys—the hiring, if need be, of a guide for a day—will put the fresh-water angler and his fresh-water tackle solidly in that new world.

I know. I began fishing as a rainbow-trout man, a plug caster, a Lake-George-lake and Adirondack-brook angler. It is quite exciting to have a one-pound trout rise to a well-directed fly, take same, and to bring same to hand net. Indeed, it is. How would you like to cast the same fly to a six-pound tarpon —and get him? It is pretty enthralling to cast a red-headed plug exactly between two spreads of lily pads and have an old lunker of a smallmouthed bass—a five-pounder—wham at the plug as you work it back. And get him. But how would you like to expose yourself and the same tackle, in an identical rowboat—to a thirty-seven-pound tarpon? Take it from me —the difference is marked and the excitement is vastly heightened by the disparity. With a mere hundred yards of line and a big fish jumping higher than your head—with barnacled piles or coral rock as a hazard instead of the stumps and snags in a pond—you will spend a remarkably beguiling afternoon fighting tarpon on casting tackle. And—well—I had a hundred-pounder on for two and a half hours once. Got him to the boat, too—and he broke off as the guide tried to gaff him. Standard black-bass tackle—and I couldn't unbend my cramped fingers for two days afterward!

Tarpon, of course, is just one kind of fish caught by fly or plug in the Miami area. Others? The devil-dancing, all-silver "ten-pounder," chiro, or ladyfish. All sorts of snappers. The groupers—a family of marine bass, coming in all sizes and colors. Channel bass, too—twenty-pounders on black-bass gear are not uncommon; elsewhere, these are called redfish, red drum, and other names. All the jacks will hit plugs if they feel like it. Barracuda lunge on them—and on flies, too. So do some of the bizarre tropical numbers. So do sharks—and *you* try to catch even a baby shark—a mere fifty-pounder—on a plug!

Then there is another, other, different realm of angling for the light-tackle addict which involves a whistling, alumi-num-colored fish called *alba vulpes* ("white wolf"), or bone-fish. He will take flies and, at times, plugs—though precious few anglers will take *him*, that way. Bonefishing is a special art and guides with inexpensive boats in and around Miami and in the Keys will show you all about it. Just to prove, more-over, that a smart bonefisherman isn't as good as he thinks he is, there is another, larger fish which frequents the still, shal-low bonefish haunts. He is a kind of pompano called a permit; and as the marlin outweighs and outpoints the sail, so the per-mit humbles the world-renowned bonefish. Any charterboat-man, hotel, or local Chamber of Commerce can put you onto the proper track for such fishing.

Of course, there are more regions, more sorts of fishing,

hundreds of fishes unmentioned here—six hundred kinds, in all, off Florida. I have barely begun to sample the situation— and my time's run out! What I had in mind to say was, principally, this: If you like to fish, try Miami fishing. If you don't like to, try it anyhow, because it may change your mind—even your life! And above all else, if you're a specialist at some sort of inland fishing, bring your favorite tackle along, by all means. For nobody has yet showed up in these parts with a style of gear for which we Miamians couldn't find all the fishing he wanted—and more, besides!

A final note to the super-wary. Everybody unfamiliar with this unique and gorgeous landscape (which is half marine-scape) seems to ask about hurricanes. The answer is— yep. Hurricanes are brewed, occasionally, a thousand or so miles from here. Most of them miss Miami. The worst one stirred up recently went to Long Island and New England. September and October are the likely months. Once in a while they do hit in other months. But we know they are coming *several days* ahead of time—so we don't get caught out fishing. And we have built all our houses, apartments, hotels and other structures to stand them. What we do, come a "blow," is to ensconce ourselves in merry parties in hotels, well provided with victuals and other refreshments, and hold our own galas until the wind dies down. A "hurricane party," as it's called, is not unlike a good convention.

If that's a worry—forget it. Indeed, Miami is designed to banish worries. And, for the angler—be he a novice or a veteran tier of his own flies—Miami is not far from Paradise.

The compleat Florida angler

I

The tourist angler generally approaches Florida in a mood of worried excitement.

He may be an old salmon man from Maine or Puget Sound; he may be a caliph among the pike and muskellunge of Wisconsin; perhaps he is a trout wizard whose waders know the upland brooks of half a dozen states; still the name of "sailfish" and the awesome reputation of the Gulf Stream will put him on his mettle.

"Tarpon" is another word calculated to shake his aplomb. Quite often, at about the point in his drive south at which

Spanish moss begins to dangle from the trees, he bolsters up his intrepidity by telling himself that salt-water fish are a brutish, sluggish sort and the taking of them is hardly a fine art.

The sad thing is that the tourist angler may go back home with that opinion—even after a good deal of conventional fishing. For much of the best of Florida fishing is unconventional: as sporting as any quest with rod and reel can be—or not sports fishing at all, but odd and fascinating.

Sailfish and tarpon, the standard quarry, are commonly taken from charter boats, operated by two guides in the case of the former and one or two in the case of tarpon. And while I would be a great hypocrite to disparage either sport, I would be less than honest to deny their handicaps, especially for the novice.

Consider sailfishing. The cost of chartering the boat runs from thirty to sixty-five dollars a day. The tackle supplied by the boatmen is generally designed for durability in the hands of beginners rather than for sporting qualities. Chances of getting a sailfish to hit on any given day are far less than even; chances of catching a sailfish, if it does hit—less again than that. Many anglers have trolled for months without taking a sailfish. And sailfishing is not a sport for persons subject to seasickness. These conditions apply in a lesser degree (except for *mal de mer*) to the commonest forms of tarpon fishing.

A tourist angler who spends days in green-gilled queasiness and gets no fish, or who takes a sailfish on a line that would do for blue marlin, or who hunts tarpon for a week and catches nothing but jack and snook on heavy tackle—one who goes

116

home lighter by a good deal in the pocketbook but not much heavier in the creel—will hold a dim opinion of Florida's piscatorial possibilities. And one who thinks that the beginning and the end of Florida fishing lies in the conventional, guided trips, together with the bottom-fishing which one observes from every bridge and even from front yards, has missed endless adventures.

Suppose you are such a tourist: an old black bass and pickerel man say, with your eye on Florida. Naturally you leave the bait-casting rods at home. The two-ounce tip, the hundred yards of twelve-pound test line, your favorite bass plugs—in Florida? In the ocean? Crazy, you are sure. So you fondly store them away—and make one of the major blunders of your life.

Down around the end of Florida lie the Keys—accessible by a dramatic highway—and around the Keys lie thousands of square miles of water—some of it only a foot deep, very little of it over your head. At a hundred spots along the road you can rent an outboard motorboat. Then with your bass tackle (and only one change: a wire leader for the gut you may have used) you are set for a style of angling with which you are familiar. In a sense, that is. You are set for lake-calm water, warm sun, shore line with coves and weed beds, fallen trees, channels and holes—all of them ideal for a well-aimed plug.

You run your boat over toward some rotted pilings off shore—a spot where a pickerel might hang out in fresh water. You cast, and work your plug. From here on I leave you to yourself—with these hints:

Plug casting is tied, in my own mind, with trolling for the great game fishes, as top fun in salt-water angling.

Your cast may bring a rushing hit that knocks the plug into the air—and a second hit which takes it under water. You may find yourself engaged in a hard fight that resembles the battle of a smallmouth bass—and finally bringing in a perchlike fish of one, two, six, even eight pounds—which will prove to be a member of the snapper family. I think you will agree that a snapper on a plug is the equal of a bass—to fight—or to eat!

But it may not have been a snapper that was lying in the shadow of those piles. Could have been a snook—which is a pike-like character. Or a sea trout. Or a jack—and a minor jack on a casting rod furnishes a very interesting ten minutes.

Suppose though it is a twenty-pound jack. That ten minutes will stretch into half an hour—or an hour—of very hard, fast fishing, before you, or the jack, gets the decision. Snapper? Snook? Trout? Jack? Mister, you have only begun to cast.

Could be a barracuda longer than your leg—and I recommend this guy, on casting tackle, to my muskellunge colleagues. Could be a grouper. Or a ladyfish, also called Chiro—which pinwheels and jitterbugs in the air like the fastest rainbow—and ladyfish grow up to be ten-pounders. That cast might attract any of a score more species which there isn't space to list here—and it is also a fine way to locate and make contact with a tarpon.

I hold, with considerable expert backing, that no man's fishing days are complete until he has attached himself to twenty or thirty or forty pounds of tarpon via a rod intended

118

for black bass. Standing in a rowboat, with his fish leaping higher than his head or running away like something out of a roman candle—and with only a hundred yards of line and the drag of his own thumb between himself and a shellacking—an angler will learn things about tarpon that are unknown to those who go after them with heavy rods, guides, large boats, strip baits, and other accessories.

Of course, if you are the perennially unlucky angler, that cast up to the pilings—or the hundredth after it—may be picked up by a shark. Or possibly by a three-hundred-pound jewfish. Or maybe a tarpon as heavy as yourself will grab your plug, feel its hooks, and start across the Gulf of Mexico by the air route.

Against such common extremities, the Florida caster carries a good supply of plugs along—and several extra lines. Furthermore, the Florida caster is sometimes embarrassed by a strike—and a catch—that is not in the finny league. Among the critters taken thus inadvertently are terns, gulls, pelicans, turtles, alligators, crocodiles, and rattlesnakes.

Reeling a pelican down from the sky is quite an experience, I guarantee—and how to turn loose an alligator is a problem never encountered in northern ponds.

Now get a grip on your chair and consider this: all the fish just mentioned, and the many more implied, take flies.

Your old salmon rod or the delicate favorite with which you pursue brook trout may also be imported to the Keys and when you get them out, no one will laugh. People may think you are piscatorially foolhardy but they will also assume you are among that rare and dangerously living breed, the salt-

water wet- or dry-fly angler. A small tarpon on a trout rod—or
a nice snapper—but I think all fly fishermen get the idea.

The fresh-water angler usually casts into likely *places*. But
in Florida's vast reaches of fish-thick "flats"—the angler often
sees his fish and stalks it—casting to his quarry personally, as
it lies, swims or feeds, plainly visible in the gin-clear water.
Such fishing is like hunting.

Barracuda, for instance, are often to be seen before they
are heard from—and more than once I have watched a casting
wizard of a lake or river region get buck fever as he tried to
aim his plug at five feet of sabre-toothed malice leering at him
from a quiet nook forty yards off.

Jacks, which travel in schools, and which feed with a roaring splash like fifty women beating fifty rugs in the water,
are among the fishes that may be taken by this sort of dead aim.

In my Florida home, on the Bay, I kept a casting rod with
a plug ready to fire hanging on the front porch. Often, while
deep in the production of literature (or as near as I could get
to same), I would hear the roaring splash of jacks in the water
outside, rush downstairs, grab the rod, cast from my front lawn,
and enjoy the next quarter hour in nonliterary excitements.
At night, ladyfish feed on shrimp with a surging surface break
—and the rod on my porch was handy for that too.

Bonefish occasionally—and, once in a great while, permit
—take plugs. These are fish which feed in shallow water, showing caudal and dorsal fins as they do so, and stirring up mud.
They too are stalked by rowboat or even by an angler in waders. Crab, shrimp, bits of conch, and the like, are the proper
bait for them—but it is no mistake to try a cast at one when

you encounter him, excepting of course for the tackle risk involved.

Bonefish and permit are commonly alleged to be the fastest fish alive; fishing for them gives thousands of savvy anglers an extended, slap-happy, old age; it is a cult—but anybody with ambition and a few bucks can join the cult.

The channel bass, alias, redfish, alias red drum, is a potent swimmer who often grows up to weigh twenty-odd pounds, and he too haunts the shallows and feeds nose-down, tail-up— so that he may be approached cautiously by poling or rowing and set into violent motion by feeding him a plug with an easy cast.

To stalk the channel bass is to enjoy a particular sport. On reddish, greenish or violet banks, where an incoming tide provides inches of water enough to float his skiff, the hunter prowls like a man with a gun. He takes care not to flush his game. And once a redfish is spotted—once the cast is made and the plug taken—a contest follows in which, as a rule, the angler has his fish in sight the whole time—and, no doubt, the fish has the angler in *his* alarmed view.

II

Some of my friends are experimenters and of these one is very lazy. It is about a hundred and eighty miles from Miami to Key West over the famed "Highway That Goes to Sea." This thoroughfare, besides furnishing some of the most dazzling marinescapes in the world, crosses many scores of bridges—the shortest of which is a few feet across, the longest seven miles. These bridges connect the Keys and carry the road over such waters as we have just been discussing. Plain bottom-fishing with shrimp for bait provides most bridges with a quota of anglers. My lazy friend, who does not cast but who likes to troll, realizing that the running tide would keep his bait clear of the bridge bastions, now carries a bicycle in his car. It is his practice to rig up a bait, drop it over the bridge rail, mount his bike, and ride sedately along the rail, trolling. He has caught a good many fish in that fashion—but he has one problem: when he hooks a big one a mile or so from the shore end of a bridge, he has to battle it the long way back before he can land it—for the line he uses will lift nothing over twelve pounds.

Another gentleman, known personally to me, conceived the notion—doubtless on a day when fishing was slow—of looking for them in an autogyro and harpooning them from the wing of same. It was some time ago—and I presume that today he would employ a helicopter; but he did manage to harpoon a shark, several 'cudas, and one loggerhead turtle—all of which were retrieved by a boat following below. This method, though interesting, is expensive and somewhat hazardous. I have heard suggestions made for trolling from blimps—and the blimp which takes passengers for a sky ride from Miami's causeway uses its shadow to scare and pursue porpoises and sharks. But, again, the blimp angler would run the risk of hanging a fish that would pull the blimp down, rather than the fish up.

An editor I know once told me of some Florida boys who were taking largemouth black bass in unlikely waters by a method which, again, has certain hazards, but the appeal of novelty. The boys attracted the bass by catching several live bumblebees, putting them in a one-gallon glass jug, and weighting the jug so that it descended to bottom. There the flying about of the bees brought the bass and the lowered baits did the rest. The editor, however, did not tell me how to catch bumblebees safely.

In my own way, I have discovered a means of initiating Florida novitiates to the fish-teeming facts of life in that area. On my front lawn stood a large Australian pine. To this I affixed a long sash cord. On the far end of that I put a cable leader and a large hook. Near the tree end of this line, I took up a couple of yards of slack and tied in it a bundle of eight heavy door springs. This rig, in other words, was a set line—and the springs were to give it play in the event of a strike. For bait I used a whole crawfish tail or a whole fish of half a pound or so. Under the scrutiny of scornful tourists, friends, and new arrivals, I would tie a heavy sinker to my rig and toss it overboard from my sea wall. I would then fix an elephant bell, which someone had brought me from India, to the tree end of the line. Then I would go about my business.

Bear in mind that the rig lay in water which surrounded a suburban tropical community—a place where people swam, aquaplaned, and bottom-fished for grunts. Often I have been interrupted at dinner, or during a bridge game, or even in my slumbers at night, by the melodious chiming of the elephant bell. Then, with my skeptical guests, I have gone out and battled, on my own lawn, two-hundred-pound sharks and rays as heavy—both leopard and stingaree. Furthermore, on half a dozen occasions, this powerful rig has been snapped and carried away by—what? I don't know. Enormous sharks, perhaps. Big jewfish. Something. Don't ask me. When an unseen fish gets away in Florida—even in the middle of a city, it could be a lot of things.

Harpooning fish in lakes, rivers, and brooks is regarded as a tame, even unsportsmanlike, activity. A harpooning expedition around the Florida Keys at night—is something else. A rowboat will do; a square-ended boat is better. A square-ended boat with a pipe railing is better still; the rail will keep the harpooner from falling overboard—and it is not good to fall into Florida salt waters in the dark. A gasoline or electric light is needed, with shade and reflector to throw a broad beam into the water and to shield the harpooner's gaze. An outboard motor is valuable for propulsion.

In such a craft, on a calm night, "prowling" through creeks, channels, into bays, across sand banks, coral bottom, and over the flats, a man with a fish spear for the small ones, and a good harpoon with rope and a buoy for the big ones, will find himself embarked upon one of the most fabulous experiences of his life. At night the fish are out. In the light they may be seen. As his boat moves slowly here and there he will see the salt-water kingdom and its denizens in thousands: fish of every species, color and size; sharks and rays; crabs and spiny lobsters; morays; the great, slow, but dangerous sawfish— and all the mats, millepores, fans, corals, plants and weird formations which make a tropical bottom look like jungle on some other planet. There are, I should say here, some six hundred species of fish in this territory.

124

Even the amateur spearman, when he becomes accustomed to the angle of refraction, can "strike" a fair number of fishes. I have known men to become so enthralled by this sport that they have preferred to do their "fishing" at night only. They bring in big jewfish—big sharks—and huge rays—as well as smaller specimens and the highly edible spiny lobsters. There is a primordial satisfaction in slamming home a harpoon—and a prodigious excitement in following a buoy as some monstrous fish—harpooned and "marked" by the shining can—rages through the mysterious dark. This sport is called "progging" and I have always wondered why so few engaged in it. The initial cost is small but the thrill tremendous, and a night's sport may be had for a few gallons of gasoline, once a boat is equipped.

Bottom-fishing is the simplest and—presumably—the tamest kind of fishing. Everywhere in Florida that water is to be found, bottom-fishermen may be seen—in rowboats, with expensive tackle—on banks and bridges, with handlines or cane poles. It is true that in Florida the bridge-and-bank angler has an opportunity to "hang" any of the great game fishes excepting those that confine themselves to the Gulf Stream. Usually, however, his intentions and his catch are confined to pan fish. But I can tell you a way to turn this pedestrian style of angling into one of the most fascinating adventures on old Ike Walton's list: take along a glass-bottomed bucket. Better still, have a glass-bottomed "well" set in your skiff.

Through the glass bottom, you can watch your bait descend—and keep an eye on it thereafter. You can see the ap-

125

proach of every fish—the nibble, the gulp. You can see the fish that approach—and do not bite. You will decide—as you watch your bait instead of as you wait to "feel" something— that there are many other fish you'd like to catch than those you are taking. And you can figure out why you're not get- ting them. The glamorous angelfishes, and the parrots—which not only have "beaks" like that bird but more and brighter col- ors than macaws—aren't being caught because your hook is far too big. Get a minnow hook and use a rice-grain-sized bait —and you may find yourself battling a three-pound angel- fish. The panorama of the bottom is yours for the price of a glass-bottomed bucket—and so is a brand new Indian sign on the fish—for you can see them, but they don't recognize you.

Such are a few of the means of fishing in Florida which— while not always conventional—are highly rewarding. And the moment you begin to fish from small boats—or along the beach —or on banks—you will spot others like yourself who will be ready, if asked, to lead you to novel methods and to new quarry. As an angler who has written a good deal about "big time" or deep-sea fishing, I was once advised by a reader to "get off my charterboat and go fishing on a bridge." Some dis- pute between that gentleman and myself arose—but I was able to squelch him finally by advising him to get off his bridge and fish *under it*. He hadn't tried that one yet.

No telling where or how you might get a fish. One pal of mine—a gent with salt water of an icy degree in his veins— not only goes goggle-fishing (diving, with goggles to make his vision clear under water, and a hand spear) but when he has speared a fish he rides up to it hand-over-hand on the spear line and wrestles it to the surface. He has done this with fifty-pound amberjacks—turning their heads up by sheer muscle and thus forcing the frantic fish to carry itself and the man on its back to the top. And he has done it out on the big reefs, amidst the twenty-foot sharks and the barracudas. If you are confident in yourself, strong, and don't give a damn what happens—there's one you might try.

Fishing in a chartered boat with expert guides is fun. A blue marlin of several hundred pounds on a rod and reel provides a degree of exhilaration difficult to understand. But, as I have said, the billfish—even the sails—don't bite every minute. It took me six years of trying to get one blue marlin and I lost eight in that period before we had my first baby in the boat. Still—if the sailfish aren't running—king mackerel and bonita will give you plenty of excitement.

One last tip—about that casting rod. Take it along on the charterboat if you go to the Gulf Stream. Maybe you'll feel sillier than a man carrying a small fire extinguisher to Hell—but take it. If you happen to run into a school of little dolphin—or a school of baby bonitas—you can settle for yourself the age-old argument: Which is stronger, pound for pound—a sea fish or a fresh-water fish. Cast a feather into the school—and then make up your own mind.

Me, I won't tell you. There are some places where even a bold man doesn't care to stick out his neck. I just say—take that casting rod along. After all, I know one guy—just one, though—who caught a sailfish on a salmon rod. But I know three or four who have caught sailfish on surf-casting tackle from piers. When you go to Florida—fish in the charterboat, Chamber of Commerce, newsreel style, if you like. But if you can't for one reason or another, don't be discouraged. Just remember that a string tied to your big toe, while you nap on a bank, can get you supper—or even take your toe off.

Nomads of the sea

It takes a lot of fisherman to catch a mako shark. It takes a couple of extra men, as a rule, to boat a mako, after an angler has brought it alongside. The tearing teeth and snatching jaws of the fabled Jabberwock had nothing on the mako: it moves like a beam of light and its mouth is loaded with ivory railroad spikes. A baby mako will cruise up to a hooked tuna and take out a hunk as big as a horse's head. And a live mako in a boat is something like a live crocodile—but possibly crocs are safer. So it takes a good deal more than "a lot of fisherman" to hook, fight *and boat* a mako shark out in the Gulf Stream—alone!

It is among the accomplishments of Captain Crawford Edmund Wall—better known as "Eddie" Wall—skipper of the yacht *Playmate* and one of the celebrated sea rovers who make up that group of guides which, off and on and more or less, is based in Miami and Miami Beach, Florida.

He tells the story modestly enough; I've heard men make more to-do over a three-pound brook trout. In those days, Eddie was in the automobile business and he fished entirely for fun. He had his own boat and he frequently ran out alone, setting a rod in a socket, steering, and keeping one eye on the course, the other on the flickering bait.

"I saw it was a mako before it hit," he said, "and I knew I was in for a battle. I killed the motor and ran back and grabbed the rod. A mouthful of teeth consumed my bait—and I sat down in the wicker chair I had for fighting. During the next hour or so that mako and I used up a lot of the ocean— he jumped plenty of times—but eventually I began to get him up to the boat. That was the part that worried me. I had only a little gaff—and I didn't want my arm to go where my bait already was. When I thought he was really worn down—I got up, grabbed my leader, set my rod back in the socket, and began the boating operation."

His eyes, at this point, are likely to glimmer. "Took me longer to get a tail rope around him and heave him aboard than the fight on the rod and reel. He was everywhere. Forward, after, under the boat, in the air—and I was everywhere with him, except overboard. Finally, though, I did get a line on him—and finally I managed to heave him in. Then I took my billy and sort of stalked him until I could knock him out."

How big was that mako? Eddie doesn't remember! Somewhere between two and three hundred pounds.

He doesn't remember, perhaps, because that was his fish and because it was just for his own fun—not business. Or, perhaps, because he has boated so many bigger ones in the intervening years—as a professional fishing guide. But it could be that he doesn't remember on purpose: Eddie Wall is an exceedingly modest guy. There are some blowhards among the world-famed charterboatmen—some who, in recounting their adventures in far places, could out-spout whales. But the majority of them are quiet men—modest men—men with a lot of character in their faces. It takes character to be a deep-sea fisherman. It takes skill and infinite patience. The biggest ones really do get away—invariably—and that makes for a kind of humility. It also takes a rugged man—physically; and there are times in the trade when it takes a large amount of internal ruggedness, too.

At night off Chile—when the sea is running big, the dark is like a closet, only the water shines—with phosphorescence —and when your customer is taking giant squid aboard, for sport. Squid with tremendous tentacles and tearing beaks. Or during some gray dawn, in unfished waters, when an unknown hulk heaves clear near by—but I am getting ahead of myself.

Most people think of a deep-sea-fishing guide as a man who, however glamorous his occupation, is pretty much attached to one dock and the cruising radius of his boat. A Jersey fisherman is a Jersey fisherman in the common view—and a Florida guide patrols his own offshore section of that state. But there is a great and a growing brotherhood of fishing guides who have dragged baits farther than the distance covered by Magellan's famed expedition—and in the same, exotic seas. Even the ordinary boatman, moreover, is likely to be no one-port sailor. The winter may find him at his home berth in Miami. But summer may see him tied up in Jersey or Maine. He may be found guiding on board a commercial boat—temporarily rigged for sports fishing—in distant Nova Scotia. And in winter, he may not see much of Miami. He may see more of the Florida Keys—or the Bahamas. He may do some fishing off Cuba. He may push down into the West Indies.

As these lines are being written, the famed Tommy Gifford, for instance—who has tossed his well-made baits into half the salt water on earth—is doing some experimental big-game fishing off Jamaica. Bill Hatch—the dean of all world-ranging guides—just happens to be at home—in Miami—for the moment. Eddie Wall's berth is empty, now, though: he's in Bimini. And Eddie Wall is a gentleman of parts who has guided in many parts—an excellent example of the increasing fraternity of guides who think of a place to fish not as a given lake, or a certain river, a stretch of coast, or a set of keys, but any spot on earth where there's open salt water.

Well over six feet, with a good, jutting jaw and the clear eyes common in seafaring men, Eddie is of an unguessable age. His look is that of a man with many dramatic years behind—and many, many more, equally dramatic—stretched out ahead. The best clue to his age is his mate—a powerhouse youngster named Gene with a good war record and a passion for angling that is the base upon which a good guide is built. Gene is Eddie's son. There is no good way to tell, by his mild and easy way of talking, where Eddie Wall originated. It was Alabama. But when he thinks of the places where fish have taken him, he thinks of all the waters around Florida, of the Florida Keys and the Bahamas and the West Indies, of Maine and Nova Scotia, of the sea off Georgia, of France and Italy and the north coast of Africa—and, especially—of a lonely little bunch of rocks in the South Atlantic.

He hasn't been in the Pacific—yet.

Sea nomads like Eddie have various means of getting around. Some take their own boats up and down the inland waterway on the east coast of the United States every year— fishing north in summer, south in winter. Others are hired to go on trips to far-off places, where their guiding knowledge is added to the knowledge of local boatmen. A commercial fisherman in Nova Scotia, for example, may own a whaleboat, or the equivalent, in which a sports fisherman may set up a fighting chair. But—until fairly recently—most Nova Scotians had no idea how to go after monster fish with such trivial tackle as rods, reels and linen lines.

Eddie has assisted professionally on numerous such expeditions. Tuna and broadbill swordfish are the quarry along the cold and foggy coasts of Canada. The angler, the boatman, and the guide go out in the gray dawns to the edge of a tidal rip and pour overboard ground-up bait to attract tuna. This is called "chumming" and, when the shapes of the tuna appear in the water or when "boils" made by their mighty tails break

133

soundlessly on the sea-surface—a baited hook is slipped into the stream of chum. A tuna is allowed to take a lot of line while it swallows such a bait. Then the drag is thrown on, the angler strikes, and one of the hardest, most dogged of sea battles is on. Only those who have tried it fully appreciate the sensation.

When a tuna hits, when it begins its celebrated initial run, an angler feels that he has inadvertently hooked into a passing express train. If the water is deep and the tuna sounds, he feels as if he had foul-hooked an elevator that had broken its cable. He sits with a rod—like any kid fishing in a pond—while, however, five or six (or more) hundred pounds of powerful fish is diving like an upended rocket, farther below him, perhaps, than the distance from the top of Manhattan's Empire State Building to the sidewalk! Even *twice* as far!

It is a most peculiar experience—exhilarating and also somewhat alarming. This writer has experienced it many times —most recently, only days ago, and on Eddie Wall's *Playmate,* off Bimini. And let the bass or trout fisherman reflect that the tuna fisherman has not only the familiar problems of currents and rocks to contend with—as well as the problem of bringing in a fish that weighs not five pounds but five hundred and has run out not fifty yards of line but a thousand—but the further problem of sharks! For a hooked tuna is an invitation to a hungry shark. Many a time, shark and angler divide the fish. And many another time only the utmost effort brings the fish to boat ahead of menacing shark-attack. Indeed, the last minutes and yards of a tuna scrap may be accompanied by yells,

boat-beatings, hat-wavings, cushion-throwings and rifle fusil-
lades aimed to discourage sharks, while the angler concludes
his mission.

Tuna, however, taken north or south, in the seething
pearliness of a Nova Scotia fog or the hot glare of the Bahamas sun, are not Eddie's top fish. And neither are mako
sharks. "The king of them all," he says, thinking of his northern
experiences, is the "broadbill swordfish. Blue marlin"—he hes-
itates and shakes his head—"blue marlin are sure spectacular.
As a matter of fact, the longest I ever had a customer on a fish
was only four hours—and that was a marlin." Anybody who
has fought a big fish for four hours may be inclined to resent
the "only." I have. I do. But Eddie shakes his head. "Still—for
speed and power—for something I can't give a name to—I
hand it to the broadbill as the fightingest fish alive."

"How big a one have you ever caught?" I asked Eddie. In
guide parlance, it should be remembered, that question refers
not to the guide himself, but his customer, client, or charterer.
It means, how big a fish has ever been caught on the guide's
boat?

"Couldn't say, exactly. We've brought in a lot of fish over
seven hundred pounds. Broadbill. A mako that went just
over seven. A lot of tunas over six hundred. On one Nova
Scotia trip—we got seven broadbills. Seven on a single trip is
pretty fair. They're hard to come by."

"What was your most surprising catch?"

He thought that over for a while—and smiled. "I can tell
you the catch that surprised the most people. Tuna."

135

"Tuna?" I didn't see that they should surprise anybody. Tuna range the waters of the earth and most sea-going men are familiar with them.

"It was over in France," Eddie explained. "Off Brittany."

We were trolling, at that moment. Trolling, ourselves, for tuna. A single, whole mullet danced in the sea behind the *Playmate*. Eddie took a look at it, and a look at Gene to be sure he was watching, too, along with a final glance up at the miniature "crow's nest" where a Bimini native boy was scanning the azure sea for signs of the big fish. Then he went on:

"The French tourist department knew it would be a good idea if big-game angling could be introduced in France. This happened last year. The Breton sardine fishermen had had plenty of trouble with tuna—getting in their nets and lousing them up—since the Year One. So the French invited Mr. Lerner to try to see what could be done—sportswise—on those tuna. Mr. Lerner asked me as a guide."

Michael Lerner, as the reader may know, is a world-famed angler, hunter, and organizer of scientific expeditions which have included a number of top fishing guides.

"Once in a while," Eddie continued, grinning at the memory, "those French sardine fishermen got a chance to harpoon a tuna. Usually it broke off. When we showed up on the Brittany coast with some rods and reels and line—a fishing chair and a couple of motors—we got just about a national raspberry. It was polite and quiet—but you could see that a lot of francs were going to be bet that we could never nail a tuna with such gear. We sort of half-converted a couple of local boats for fishing our way—and we went out with the fleet.

136

"The weather was decent—cool, though. A well torn-up net from a few days back made it plain that the tuna were around those parts. So we started to fish. Well—we got one. Got one, in spite of the fact that it was darn near impossible to maneuver the boats—our engine conked, too—and the chair-rig broke up in the fight. There was something in the nature of a celebration when we brought that fish in. Celebration and feast. Tunas are darned good eating—and the whole fishing village ate tuna that night. Furthermore—they sort of hated tunas for the net-smashing—and it was a revenge to fish one out like a trout. There was—also—the matter of future sports-fishing profits—to add to the fun."

Eddie started to go on—interrupted himself—peered at the bait—and shrugged. "Thought I saw a swirl there. Barracuda—or the like. Guess I didn't. Anyhow—we showed the town movies of big-game angling in New Zealand and Australia. Trips Mr. Lerner had made. Black-marlin fishing—and so on—in colored film. Rigged up a projector in a sardine cannery—and the whole town came to watch. No seats— they stood for two hours and they were just about as enthralled as any bunch I ever saw. Being fishermen themselves. Mrs. Lerner went out a few days later and astonished them again—by taking a tuna. In all—we got seven tunas and I guess big-game angling is officially launched in France." His tone changed slightly. "It's a white marlin."

So it was. Black bill and dark fin surged to the surface behind my tuna bait. Young Gene rushed for light tackle and, in seconds, he had a strip bait overboard. The idea was to drop it back and lure the marlin to take it instead of the tuna bait.

This particular white, unfortunately, was too hungry to dally. He grabbed the whole mullet, yanked the line out of the outrigger, and started off. When the line came tight, I had him—on the thirty-nine-thread line we were using for tuna instead of the nine-thread line we'd quickly put over.

Tuna tackle is intended for tuna and even an eighty-pound white marlin—on such gear—has no chance. I kept the drag tight—at the point intended for a tuna strike. The hooked marlin turned away from the boat and tried to swim—but all he did was create a big wash. He couldn't even turn the reel! So he gave that up and executed a few, twisting high jumps. Then I brought him to the boat and signaled to turn him loose. It then proved, however, that this fish was wanted by the research scientists at Bimini—wanted for food for some rarer live specimens.

"What," I asked Eddie, when the boating activity died down and we had rebaited for tuna, "was your most interesting trip?"

It was the answer to that question which, in my opinion, makes Eddie Wall uniquely interesting among the sea-roving guides.

"You know where the Ascension Isles are?" he asked.

I did know.

"A Godforsaken heap of rocks between South America and Africa, belonging to Great Britain. Before the war it had been merely a cable station; perhaps a dozen people had lived there in near-intolerable loneliness. High, rocky shores, two scraps of beach, no harbors but only the dubious lea of the

rock pile itself, wind blowing all day and all night, seas smashing eternally, dust scouring the naked landscape, millions of
birds using it as a rookery, and millions of turtles climbing
over each other and digging up each other's eggs when they
came in on the heavy seas and tried to use the two inadequate
beaches for breeding. That was Ascension before the war—
just about the last stop at the End of Time. But, during the
war, an airfield had been blasted and bulldozed on this bit-
ter land. It had become an intensely busy station on the trans-
atlantic flyways. It was also used as a rest area. Thousands upon
thousands of American soldiers came to know endless months
of service upon this sea-loved epitome of desolation.

"Fresh food was their problem," Eddie said. "Especially
fresh meat. It just wasn't. They knew there were fish—plenty
of fish—in the waters around the islands. But how to take
them? Seas rolling all the time. No boats available. No know-
how among thousands of men. One of the Britishers stationed
there used to get small fish—a lot of them—plug casting. But
there wasn't any tackle except his light rod—and you can't
feed umpteen thousand guys with a black-bass rod and a few
plugs. Some place! They couldn't even let the men go swimming there. The seas were so rough they knocked guys out.
And when you got stunned in those seas, you were done for—
and done for in a creepy manner. Not far offshore was a belt
—and I mean a dark, visible belt—of literally billions of black
triggerfish and they'd eat anything—even a piece of paper out
of your hand. We tried that, later. Anyhow—if a swimmer
got stunned by the seas, or fuddled, those little triggers would

eat him. They told me that three bathers were taken that way —and all they got back was the clean-picked skull of one of them. So they didn't swim at Ascension.

"Some of the big-game anglers knew about the awful rations down there—from talks with Army people—and from flying to the war by way of the place. They thought guides like myself could find out how to get those offshore fish—and it turned out that the Government sent me down to investigate the situation.

"Remember the wartime shortages? Fishing tackle was so short it wasn't. I rummaged over half the country collecting gear. I got flown down there, finally, with about three hundred pounds of stuff. The Navy had left an old boat on shore there —a forty-five-footer of the commercial swordfish type. We got her in condition and took her out to sea. I had ten men assigned to me by the Army. Not one was a fisherman of any sort.

"Anyhow—the first crack, we hit Allison tuna. They're related to the ones we're looking for today—but smaller—and gaudier. Lot of yellow on them. Run from a hundred to two-seventy-five pounds. Well—we marked the ledge where we found the fish with a buoy. To anchor that, even, in the seas and currents around there, we used a whole, old motor. Seven of the ten soldiers assigned me got too seasick for fishing. But three of them panned out fine.

"We began operations the next day—our buoy was about two miles offshore in sixteen fathoms. No fancy fishing. Hand lines—tough ones—gloves on your mitts—and haul 'em in as fast as you could. We four guys—the three that didn't get sick, and myself—caught eleven hundred pounds of tuna in three hours. Day after, we tried bottom-fishing closer in. They had billions of jacks down there—looked something like blue jack —but they tasted like pompano, which is about as fine an eating fish as swims. Those jacks ran from ten to twenty-five pounds—and we chummed them up—then dropped baited hooks over. We nailed fifteen hundred pounds of them in one day—the four of us."

Eddie paused and shook his head slowly. "If you've never been stuck on a dusty, barren island for months, without fresh meat, you can't imagine the effect of that fishing. I never saw people eat fish like that in my life—and never will again. Officers and men. Anyhow—I got the 'commercial fishing' operation set up—and from then on, there was fresh fish on the Ascension menu. I went back there later with more gear— spent about three months on the job, all told. And I'd like to go back again some day—to sports fish. Not just for the jacks and the Allison tunas. There were other fish around there— red-hot fish—too hard to try for, when you needed meat so badly. But the shark-mangled remains of one wahoo that some-body caught weighed a hundred and fifty pounds!" He looked at the sea over the stern of the *Playmate*. "An eighty-pounder is a whopper, around Bimini here."

Later, I learned that Eddie was supposed to be on a "per diem" basis while he did this astonishing and novel war job. Only, somehow, he never collected. And I also found out that, to get the tackle he thought the boys needed on Ascension, he spent a lot of his own money. Only, he never turned in a bill. His son Gene was in uniform; he was doing his bit to help the Wall war record.

Some fishermen and fishing spots

Any readers of this book who passed dreary weeks on Ascension—and there will be many—if they recall fresh fish as a precious break in Army rations—ought to offer up a silent vote of thanks to Captain Eddie Wall. It takes the kind of man who will hook, fight and boat a mako shark—alone and for fun—to make the kind who can pioneer far and foreign seas in jerry-made boats for the benefit of his hungry countrymen.

Eddie told me that story, and was adding a few minor details, when our first tuna struck. As was said earlier, the angler—in this case myself—felt as if he was trying to stop an elevator that had broken loose in the shafts of something higher than the Empire State Building. And when, a half hour later, the thousandth violent heave by your correspondent pulled the hook out of said tuna, Eddie was more disappointed than I. After all, I'd caught tunas before. And furthermore—though I didn't mention it to Eddie—I was beginning to wonder whether I really wanted to fight that fish to the end or not. Anybody who has battled a tuna will ask himself the same question after half an hour or so. After a couple of hours, he may have a quite definite opinion about his folly.

At this moment (1950), Eddie Wall's guiding has an other-than-sporting aspect. He and his son and their *Playmate* are assisting in the collection of specimens which are being used to stock the extraordinary pens of the Lerner Marine Laboratory in Bimini. This laboratory—a field station of the American Museum of Natural History—maintains alive in stockades in the harbor such monstrosities as manta rays. They contain the first dolphins, so far as are known, that have ever lived in captivity. Giant tuna and white marlin are on the list of fishes

142

wanted alive by the scientists; and Captain Wall, along with the famed Bill Hatch and Doug Osborne—two more of the world-traveled guides—have been assisting in the hunt.

Not every man is able to troll in the deep, blue water for the whoppers. This has occasioned some envy on the part of those who cannot enjoy the sport. And the envy has led to some deprecation of deep-sea fishing. It needn't do so. Eddie Wall can tell you why.

"A man with unlimited time and funds naturally has the best chance at a big fish," he says. "But luck enters into the proposition more than you might expect. In the fifteen years I've been a guide, for instance, I've fished men who could afford it for weeks—and seen them come to the end of long charters without a spectacular catch. But I've also been chartered—over and over again—by, say, three or four guys who split the costs and went out for a single day—and broke some record or other!

"Anybody can afford a quarter of a day's charter once in a while—and anybody who has a line in the sea is even with everybody else—however many days the other guys may have been at it. You know. Fishing is like flipping a penny and having it come up heads a hundred times straight. The odds that it will come heads the next flip are—still—fifty-fifty. I've seen —as a matter of fact—one Florida record—for broadbill— busted by a man who went out for a half day. He had never fished before. And he never went again. Guess he thought he could rest on his laurels from there on in."

There's another thing. The enjoyment of fishing is relative. The reader has noted that the taking of a fish—even a big one like a white marlin—on tackle meant for something still bigger—isn't sport at all. It is cold assassination. So the man with the fly rod in the rowboat enjoys a prospect of excitement that, relatively, is no different from that experienced by the man with heavy tackle in the stern of a cruiser. Here, again, Eddie Wall may be cited as a super-authority.

"Personally," he says, "I like all kinds of fishing. In fact, in some ways, I like plug casting and fly casting best. At least —when I take a day off, maybe a couple of times a year, I always load my car with light tackle—fly rods, casting rods, spinning gear—and drive out along the canals. Or I may take an outboard around the Cape—after some little tarpon or, maybe, snook and jacks. Boy!"

Busman's holiday! And Everyman's sport.

All over the world there are fishermen wondering what lies in the waters they now have no way to reach. All over the world there are anglers who have seen something they couldn't identify and who desperately long to boat a specimen of it. In Fiji and the Philippines, in New Zealand and in Ceylon, in Capetown and in Rio. Here and there, around the world, men are making plans to find out what that lost monster was—and how to take it. That kind of curiosity led to the discovery that big squid can be caught on rod and reel off Chile, for example. It led to the taking of the first marlin on sports tackle, and the first sailfish. It led, long ago, to that famous matter of the eating of the first oyster. And all over the United States, as well as some other countries, there are guides ready to go anywhere and see what's what.

Guides to whom no spot is too remote, if big fish are ru-

144

mored to live there. Guides to whom no fishing method is too dizzy to try—so long as it conforms with the rules of good sportsmanship. Guides who, even in the normal course of events, fish by summer and winter from harbors a couple of thousand miles apart. Born fishermen who take their pride and their excitement in fish caught by their customers. Nomads of the sea—they turn strange legends into fishing feats that are, still, of legendary proportions. And wherever they hit the jack pot—more anglers come in their wake—you, perhaps, and I. The widespread notion that pioneering ceased years back is plain silly—when you consider the sea.

The IGFA

There is probably no more thrill-packed sports document in existence than the World Record Chart of the International Game Fish Association. All it is, in actual fact, is a printed table, about the size of an automobile road map, which lists the various marine game fish of the world and the biggest of each species that has been taken, so far as is known, on a variety of graduated sizes of tackle. But, by implication, it is the story of the top achievements in a great sport—a summary of daring and unusual episodes in the lives of outdoor men and women. Often enough, furthermore, the tales of the fish that were almost records, or almost eligible—are wilder and stranger than the accounts of the world-beaters.

Imagine, for instance, the predicament of Mr. X—a noted sports angler and light-tackle expert—trolling for sailfish off Mexico in the Pacific with his equally renowned friend, Mr. Y. Mr. X is using three-thread line, which has a breaking strain of just nine pounds. Mr. Y's six-thread line will break under a strain of eighteen pounds. A sailfish—a monster—appears behind the baits: huge, cobalt dorsal fin—slicing black bill. It takes Mr. X's bait—but before Mr. X can strike, the sail shoots across the wake of the fishing cruiser and also gulps Mr. Y's bait.

Then, having cleaned up the visible viands, the sailfish runs. Both lines come tight. Both reels scream.

These anglers are expert. They know the fish is a whopper, and that it may even be a record. But it is much more likely to be a record on the lighter of the two lines. So Mr. Y immediately tightens his reel-drag to a point which causes his six-thread line to snap. Thereafter, Mr. X is solely attached to the giant and he begins the long, dramatic, yet cautious battle by which a fish that weighs more than a hundred pounds is sometimes caught on a line that will break if, at any time, more than nine pounds of stress is put on it. In due course, Mr. X boats the fish. It is rushed to shore and weighed. The World Record Chart is consulted. Sure enough—this sail is bigger than anything shown for tackle of the class used. It's a world record—*if* the judges decide it was fairly caught.

An International Game Fish Association (or "IGFA") application blank is filled out, question by question. It is signed by witnesses and by a weighmaster and notarized. A sample of the line used is sent with the application to IGFA headquarters at the American Museum of Natural History in New York City. And Mr. X gets the decision in due course.

One of the rules makes it plain that the angler must hook and fight his fish *unaided* and without interference. The fact that his sailfish was attached, even if only for seconds, both to a three-thread line and to a six-thread line means that a single angler did not do every bit of the "catching" of the fish. It means that the sailfish fought not only against Mr. X's line but also against the hook, bait and dragging broken line of Mr. Y. It *may* have been easier for Mr. X to hook the fish in the moment when Mr. Y tightened his drag and broke his line. A fine feat of angling—and a noble gesture on the part of Mr. Y to break his line—a world-record-*size* sailfish—but one not caught quite according to Hoyle, wherefore, no record.

Sometimes it goes the other way. Somebody who has never been deep-sea fishing before in his (or her) life is taken out for a day's trolling by a friend. The novice has a tremendous strike—of he knows not what—and hangs on. Directions and exhortations come from friend and boatmen. The battle rages for minutes, for hours. The inexperienced angler brings his quarry to boat. It is weighed, the chart is examined, and the application filed. Then—good news! More than one world record is held by a "first time" fisherman—which goes to show that luck is part of the game.

Luck isn't all. On two different occasions I have seen average anglers deliberately go after a world record in a certain class of tackle, for a particular species of fish—and get it!

How come? The explanation is simple. Even after years of record-keeping, on various sizes of tackle and for various rather common species of fishes, the standing entry may be nothing much as the breed goes—or there may be no entry at all. The IGFA will not list just *any* fish as a world record. You need a king-sized specimen for the tackle you use, to get on the Big Board. But, in the classifications where there is no entry, or where the entry is not notably huge, all you need is patience and determination—along with a modicum of good fortune— to "knock off" the incumbent record or to fill in the blank space. Light-tackle records, especially, often change because big-fish angling on light tackle is still a comparatively new sport. Everybody has a chance!

There is no end to the dilemmas of the judges. Here's one on which there has been argument but no decision: Is a fish that jumps into the boat fair caught? This writer holds that it is not. But at least one of the most exacting anglers in the land holds that if you hook a fish foolish enough thus to boat himself, and if he happens to be of record size, it's your good luck. There has been no decision on the matter because no fish of record size has yet jumped aboard. But plenty of big ones, in their wild, pinwheel leaps, have come down not in the sea but on the deck. I have had five hundred pounds of marlin jump higher than my head within six feet of the gunwale—frightening everybody with the expectation that the next leap might end amongst ourselves. There are authentic instances of arms and legs broken by tarpon that leaped into small boats and continued their frenetic activities in the midst of people—not purposely, but by accident or miscalculation.

So it is almost certain that someday an application will come in for a fish "caught" in that way—and the IGFA executive committee will have to decide the matter.

A "mutilated" fish is not eligible for a record. And some of the biggest fish caught, unfortunately, are mutilated. Their very size nearly always means that the fight will be extra long. That, in turn, spells steadily increasing peril of the marine angler's greatest menace: shark. A fish may be nearly beaten and very tired—but not yet so weary that the angler can bring him to gaff. Yet when a marauding shark appears, the hooked fish may be unable to keep clear. The result is an attack—an attack which often kills and always weakens the game fish; hence, when it is brought mutilated to boat, it is not considered fair caught. The angler must bring in a whole fish.

But what about this one? Recently, an official of the IGFA was called by ship-to-shore phone for a ruling. An anguished competitor in a tournament has just boated a tuna which would put himself and his team in the lead—if it was eligible. But its eligibility was contested because that particular tuna had been bitten, apparently by a shark, though not during the battle. The bites were *weeks old* and pretty well healed. Did they count against the angler—or was that natural misfortune of the fish an acceptable "break" which made it, perhaps, easier for the fisherman to boat his quarry?

I was the official called. I didn't have to get a ruling made; for the IGFA offers ruling *only* in the question of applications for world records. I explained that fact. The frantic fishermen implored me, then, to get an "unofficial opinion"—because, he said, the tournament judges had been unwilling to commit themselves and feeling about the matter was intense. By long distance and local phone, by wire and letter, I hurriedly got together some entirely unofficial opinions, but before I could offer them, the tournament committee reached what the IGFA experts had agreed was probably the best possible decision:

If it was established that the old injuries no longer materially weakened the tuna, it should be regarded as fair caught. (Fish, after all, have diseases. They even have cancer. And there is no rule against a world record for a sick fish; a health card is not part of the requirements.) But if the old mutilations were such as still to weaken the tuna, it was generally, though not unanimously, felt that the catch should be disqualified.

Disqualifications are sometimes humanly hard to make. A magnificent marlin was taken, not long ago, on quite light tackle, by a war veteran who was physically handicapped. He had fought the fish *all day*. But at one point, for a period of about ten minutes, he had surrendered the rod to a boat mate. The marlin was heavy enough for a record. But the rule says that the record maker must have caught his fish alone. Other physically handicapped men have made records. There is an authentic account of the taking of a swordfish *by a woman* after a singlehanded, unbroken battle of *more than thirty hours!* Feats of that sort—feats sometimes doubted by persons who believe that a harpoon rather than a rod and reel is the suitable gear for big-fish fishing—show why the IGFA is uncompromising.

The rules have to be absolute. Any fisherman (like your reporter, for an example) who has fought fish through the heat of day into the dark of night, through tumultuous storms on seas higher than his cruiser was long, in hard rains and icy gales and lightning, drifting far from shore in the battle—any such fisherman—knows that the iron-clad rules of the IGFA are his best protection. A sport without rules is not a sport— it's a racket. With firm rules—and experts to judge—the angler knows that no one will get away with short cuts to an achievement that he has found so difficult and so challenging. Members of the executive committee of the IGFA—of which I'm one—are not, in any case, eligible to hold world records. But it is reassuring for them—as for all fishermen—to realize that every imaginable human effort is made to rule out gypping from big-game angling.

How did such an organization come about? What is the IGFA? Thereon—as always, when the subject is fishing—hangs a tale.

A decade or so ago, the question of who caught what biggest fish on which tackle was wide open. The American Museum of Natural History kept a haphazard list of so-called "world record" catches of marine fishes. But the listings were not carefully checked, the method of catch was not ordered by rules, and, while some of the "records" in this list were turned in by famed and reliable anglers, others were the casual claims of gentlemen who may have used harpoons instead of rods and reels or may perhaps have shot their fish after they had been hooked. Among the anglers, Mr. Zane Grey and Mr. Michael Lerner—fishermen who had tossed baits into some of the remotest, giant-haunted seas on earth—had made entries.

In England, where the inland art and skill of Izaak Walton began the long, thrill-spangled history of sports fishing, and where a Briton will go a whole hundred miles by small boat into the frigid North Atlantic for a whack at a tuna, the British Tunny Club was making an attempt to bring order out of the chaos of claimed records. In California, a tradition brought by a Texas angler had been used to set up the very high standards of several clubs—which insisted that a fish taken on line larger than twenty-four-thread (breaking strain: seventy-two pounds) wasn't worthy of notice! These pioneers made some extraordinary records on that relatively light gear. At the same time, in Australia and in New Zealand, great ranges of black marlin, of striped marlin, of mako sharks, threshers, and various other fishes had been discovered. And fishing enthusiasts in those areas, proud of their achievements and jealous of the possibility that Mother England might become the sole arbiter of records, felt that a non-British headquarters for angling would be ideal—a very fortunate feeling, for on September 3, 1939, England was at war.

In 1939, while he headed an expedition for the American Museum of Natural History to Australia, Mike Lerner fell to discussing the matter with Clive Firth—of that land down under—another noted angler. It was Mr. Firth's suggestion that Americans should devise and administer the rules. For the Australian noted a long-standing tendency of the colonies and the mother country to quarrel about everything—even about rules for fishing. Mr. Firth, aware of the feats of the Californians, of Floridians, Long Islanders and others, felt that England, along with her colonies and dominions, would accept American judgment as sporting and impartial—and without

154

starting another Revolutionary War. He thought all other nations would accept the lead of U.S.A. and Britain.

Mike Lerner (and Dr. W. K. Gregory, together with the late, famed Harry Raven and several equally noted members of that expedition) pondered the Australian's proposal on the voyage home. Mike next got in touch with leading anglers and prominent fishing clubs the world over, for opinions. They were enthusiastic. Everybody wanted to be in the game—but nobody wanted to umpire.

A bit reluctantly, Mike selected a group of deep-sea fishermen known for their skill and fairness, a number of ichthyologists and other scientists, and a few chaps like Van Campen Heilner, who had fished about everywhere and written authoritative articles and books on the subject. Included in the last category was the great Ernest Hemingway, whose sports stories have graced the pages of many a publication and are among the very best in the language, and who is a hell-for-leather nemesis of sea-lurking monsters. Later on, this writer also became an officer of that world-umpiring society. (I had, by then, written a bit about sea fishing and wet a line here and there—though I shall remain to my dying day a tyro at fishing compared with Mike or Van or Ernest or a hundred other men known personally to me and thousands who exist unknown.)

Today, the IGFA supplies to anyone on request printed rules for standard tackle and "fair" fishing methods. The IGFA also supplies forms to be filled in by anybody claiming a world record—forms which include directions on how to measure fish properly and which demand the exact data on the kind of

155

line used, the type of rod, reel, number of hooks (no more than two are allowed) and so on. A snapshot of the fish and the tackle is required. So is a sample of the line actually used in making the catch; and that sample, in every case, is checked by a professional testing company. "World records" are kept in many categories, each depending upon the "breaking strain" of the line used. Thus, there is a set of world records for fish taken on line that breaks at a strain of twelve pounds (or "twelve-pound test"), on twenty-pound test, thirty, fifty, eighty, and so on—with a final "All Tackle" class which lists the biggest fish caught fairly on whatever size tackle.

Today, though you belong to no fishing club, you can submit your entry simply by writing for one of the IGFA forms, filling it in properly, having it witnessed and notarized, and sending along with it a hunk of your line and a photograph.

It may seem a little far-fetched to imagine yourself taking a world-record fish on your first trip at sea, with no angling experience whatsoever—except those catfish. But the only thing that's far-fetched is our imaginary "broad-head." On the master record chart of the IGFA are *several* world records made by novice fishermen—and fisherwomen. In fact, one day while I was arranging a charter at a Miami Beach fishing dock, I saw a lady come in with what became the women's All Tackle record for Atlantic sailfish and I talked to her about the catch. It was her first—her very *first*—experience with a rod and reel in any water!

The IGFA has been in existence for more than a decade. Its reports are recognized everywhere—except in Soviet Russia, where we have no word of the fishing situation. (Doubtless, the Reds, if they took part in the perpetual, planet-wide contests, would claim *all* records in *all* classes—and refuse to furnish any proof whatsoever!) An established fishing club whose members desire it to belong to the IGFA is admitted upon application and after an examination to make sure the club is bona fide and its members are genuine sports fishermen. There are several hundred such "member clubs." In the angling centers of all civilized nations (and many that would be considered highly uncivilized), the IFGA has a "representative" who serves for the honor of the post and the love of the sport. He is available to give anybody and everybody IGFA information as well as to investigate any question that may come up about a record claim from his area.

The IGFA itself is housed in the American Museum of Natural History, on Central Park West, in New York City and is reached by all letters thus addressed. Its resident officer is Miss Francesca LaMonte, the association's secretary—and a noted ichthyologist. All other officers, representatives and so on serve without pay. There are no dues for member clubs and no charge is made for publications. The IGFA has *no* individual members, as the officials connected with the association are not, strictly speaking, "members." They hold their status merely to serve the *member clubs,* and the great sport of marine fishing. They scrutinize all claims for records. The "okay" of at least the president, a vice-president and the secretary is necessary for the acceptance of a claim as a new record. Wherever insufficient or confusing information about a catch is furnished, the secretary first asks for clarification. If that proves insufficient, a local representative is instructed to make an on-the-scene investigation.

So, frequently, men in Capetown and Queensland, in Tahiti and Chile, take trains and planes to some remote spot where a gigantic fish has been caught—or a fish spectacularly large for the type of tackle used—just to make sure a "world record" is justified. If the "local" man fails to solve a questionable situation (Was the line really twelve-pound test? Did the fish actually weigh seventy-six and a quarter pounds? Are the scales that said the marlin went over a thousand *accurate?* Was the fish gaffed according to IGFA rules—or is the rumor it was harpooned, true?), an official from the home office may start a long trek to check in person.

There is something inspiring about every sportsman and his devotion to what is, after all, a kind of "arbitrary idealism." In the ten years I've served the IGFA, I've helped with many queries and investigations and I've seldom missed one of the meetings at which the officials thresh out the hardest questions accumulated in each year. Before I served IGFA, I imagined myself something of a purist on tackle and a stickler for form and detail. But my colleagues taught me more. I've seen our newest official, Ben Crowninshield (who is one of the best anglers living today) spend *a month* over the matter of the way hooks were employed on a claimed-record catch. I've seen Mike Lerner take off for remote parts to check a detail as small. I've seen all the men in IGFA invariably do their utmost to give the angler every possible "break." But *never* have I

seen a sign of prejudice, of personal interest or motive, of anything but hard-working integrity.

Yet the problems are sometimes a strain on the judges, as
human beings. For example, not long ago, an Allison tuna
was taken in the Pacific by a lady angler who was more or less
a novice. The captain of the boat she had chartered was an old
hand. The tuna hit the bait while the rod was in a "socket"
(like the sockets that were used long ago to hold buggy-whips).
The lady angler grabbed for her rod—which fit tightly in the
socket. The tuna, meantime, had taken the bait, whirled and
was running away—no doubt feeling the hook as it ran, which,
if true, accelerated him.

At such times, even on the boats of the oldest anglers and
in the presence of the most experienced guides, anything but
calm prevails. The strike of a walloping big fish is to an angler
what a lion or an elephant in his rifle-sights is to a hunter. In
fact, it's more; for the hunter's work usually ends with that
high moment—while the angler's just commences. Think,
then, of such an instant—a big strike, a tremendous run, and a
lady unable to get her rod free of the socket, owing to its close
fit and to the pressure being exerted on it by the racing tuna.

In this crisis, to free the rod, the skipper hit it jarringly a
few times with his open hand. The lady was thereby enabled
to get the rod-butt out of the socket, carry the gear to the
fighting chair, set it in a gimbal, and go to work on the fish.
Some hours later—and what hours of combat a big tuna can
supply!—she brought the fish to the boatside where the mate
took the leader, the skipper thrust home the gaff and a "world

record" Allison tuna was boated—*if the officials of the IGFA would agree it had been fair caught.*

Now it happens that the lady in question was the wife—the handsome, photogenic, famed and charming wife—of a man of great wealth and influence. It happens that the city off which she took her big fish was very anxious to get the publicity that would ensue if a world record was made there, especially by so charming and famed a lady. But it *also* happens that the rules of the IGFA say unequivocally that the angler shall hook and fight and bring to boat his fish *unaided* and that *no one else* shall touch any part of the tackle at any time until the final moment when the leader is seized so the fish may be gaffed. On the other hand, it is well known that the IGFA officials will do their best, when the situation warrants it, to judge in favor of the angler. But they will *not* violate rules! The claim for a record was, consequently, denied.

A considerable amount of protest was made over that decision—which was reviewed at an annual meeting. Again the claim was turned down. Some of the city fathers were huffy about what they called "quibble over an outrageous technicality." But *the lady herself* did not protest at all—however much she might have liked to hold a world record. Note, *instead,* that in her affidavit she reported the captain had repeatedly struck the rod to free it. That's sportsmanship! She and they could have omitted the fact—and would certainly have been awarded the record.

But note *further* the points pondered by the IGFA officials in discussing the matter. That "jury of experts" brought out the obvious fact that if a skipper or mate is allowed to touch a rod on one occasion, a hundred skippers and mates will do more, on the next. Further, the hard, open-palmed slaps the skipper gave the rod to loosen it *may* have been the blows *that drove the hook into the tuna's mouth.* That is to say, had the lady managed to lift the rod unassisted, and started with it to the fighting chair, the tuna *might not* have been hooked and *might* have escaped! For *any* interference by a second person changes the fishing conditions. And too many skippers and mates the world over (especially when taking out inexperienced anglers) are prone to grab the rod whenever a fish rises. *Maybe* they'll hand it to tyro before the fish hits; but some will themselves make sure the fish is well hooked before turning over the tackle to the customer. That's patently unfair.

So the lady forfeited her claim—with the regret of the IGFA officers. Perhaps there ought to be a special award for "near misses" in world records and another for "extreme gallantry"—in which case the lady would be eligible for both. But the anglers who sit on the IGFA "jury" are not likely to put up such awards. For *every man-jack of them* has at the very least *nearly* boated a "world record" fish, time and again —including even me.

People cheat—occasionally. The lady who told the exact truth about her Allison tuna is far more representative—a hundred times more—than the man or woman who tries to defraud the IGFA and to be accredited a world record on a fish unfairly caught, or a fish not as big as claimed, or something of that sort.

Naturally, the IGFA relies first and foremost on the integrity of the angler. It has to. The IGFA cannot have an inspector in every boat and on every dock and beach where anybody is fishing, the world over. So you *could* catch a walloping big fish—but not a record—and photograph it along with, say, far lighter tackle than you actually used. You *could* then claim it to be heavier than the fact—and a record on, say, twelve-pound test line when you really used seventy-two-pound test. You *might* find a dockmaster and a weighmaster and other persons who would swear that your report was gospel truth. Your filled-in form and your affidavit, your photograph of your fish and of tackle you didn't use—along with your phony sample of line—*might* pass muster. You might, eventually, get word from the IGFA that you held the twelve-pound-test world record for—say—snook. The IGFA relies on the honor system since it cannot police the world.

But we officials at IGFA believe there are no violations even of the most trifling parts of the rules among the catches listed as world records. For one thing, anglers—contrary to the legend about them—tend to be more scrupulously honest than the general run of Homo sapiens. For another, the eyes that scan the photographs and read the affidavits are very expert—the eyes of trained scientists, veterans anglers. For a third factor, since honor is a jealous guardian of world records, the angler who cheats raises the hackles of *all other anglers*. And the rumor of a faked entry gets around: a man who used heavy tackle to take a fish that he claimed as a record on *light* tackle may have been seen, that day, faring forth with his *heavy* gear and *nothing else*. Somebody—some indignant angler—writes the IGFA. Investigation gets under way. And presently, the malefactor is trapped or persuaded into admitting his dishonest attempt.

Occasionally, someone who doesn't know all the IGFA rules enters a fish innocently and finds out afterward that his catch wasn't made "according to Hoyle." Perhaps his leader wire was longer than the legal limit. Possibly his guide—an unschooled native in some remote land—instead of gaffing the fish, threw a trident into it the first time it surged within spearing range. That angler will, in our experience, invariably write to withdraw his claim.

It is not the dishonesty of people but their scrupulousness which makes IGFA work fascinating. The great majority of investigations conducted by us are not owing to our suspicions about claims but to inquiries concerning the legality of a catch *made at the request of the angler himself.*

In a time in our national sports history when football and basketball and other such games have come under the pall of proven dishonor, of bribery and corruption and cheating, it is refreshing to see how ardently myriads of fishermen—fishermen in a hundred countries, fishermen of every tint of skin, fishermen who speak all the major languages—not only play the game straight but take near-universal pride in doing so. (It can be seen here that the IGFA is lucky to be housed in the American Museum of Natural History since its correspondents often use languages it takes an archaeologist or an anthropologist or some other scientist-visitor of remote regions to translate!)

Anglers are funny people. And the IGFA, being a sort of

world crossroads for anglers, is in consequence an unusual and interesting place. People drop in at IGFA for advice on where to take a next vacation or on what tackle to carry to the Celebes or Patagonia. These persons drop in again, usually, on their return—with marvelous tales of fish, seen, hooked, lost—and caught, mounted and ensconced above the mantel at home. Cablegrams come in from every quarter of the globe asking for every imaginable sort of fishing information and telling every conceivable kind of tale about fishes seen or apparently seen or reported by somebody to somebody else.

A great many travelers, foreigners in America, know *only the IGFA* when they arrive here for a visit. So they make tracks to the American Museum. Their reception is always warm. Americans voyaging into any of the sixty-odd regions overseas where IGFA has a representative or a member club, or both, have found that "I'm a fisherman" is an open-sesame to new languages, to an ideal way to make new friends and a sure means of finding new piscatorial fun. For fishermen, being philosophers, are also friendly; ninety-nine in every hundred take pride and pleasure in "hanging" a stranger on one of their local big-game beauties. The notion that anglers keep secret their "best" fishing grounds has been blown to statistical mincemeat by IGFA. Hunters may have such a selfish practice; but if so, fishermen are different.

"I know," they will say (on the shores of the Red Sea or the Yellow Sea, or the coast of Wales or Africa), "a special spot where the monsters really bite!" And then they take you there.

So—in sum—the IGFA keeps world records of marine

game fish taken according to its rules on graduated sizes of tackle. The rules have been submitted for acceptance to the member clubs; any change in them is made only after a year or so of discussion and a *vote,* majority-determined, by the member clubs—*not,* as some think, by IGFA officials. The IGFA also acts, the world over, as a sort of international good-will embassy from and to people who fish. It publishes the up-to-date rules. It publishes, from time to time, a yearbook reporting its planet-wide news. It publishes, annually, a chart of world records, brought up to date. And it has plans for extending its scope to include scientific information.

For nowhere else on earth is there such an association of human beings as that which exists amongst the membership of the IGFA member clubs: men and women by the hundreds of thousands who are familiar with fishing and the sea, fond of both and devoted to their pursuit. These people are ideally suited to collecting certain kinds of scientific information which would help enormously in filling out unknown chapters of sea knowledge. Future yearbooks will show what IGFA people can do in that respect. For in it will be a huge table, by months, of what fish may be caught where on this planet, with what baits—not just a superguide for sportsmen who want a new kind of fishing vacation but a huge survey of where the fish are, and go, *when*—that will be of great interest to science. The officers of the IGFA know that the training and the observation of sports fishermen can be put to countless other uses, of value to science. Even now, some enigmas and problems of ichthyologists in various parts of the earth are being sent to IGFA headquarters—whence they go out to appropriate clubs and persons for an answer that often overwhelms the inquiring scientists with useful data.

It is apparently a "law of human nature" that the sea hunter will become the observer, the observer an amateur naturalist and he, in turn, will take such an interest in passing on the wonders he sees to science that he becomes more than an amateur. Indeed, many anglers, like many hunters, have put aside their killing equipment and replaced it with the gear for observation and study. So the IGFA hopes and expects, in the years to come, to be increasingly not a sports society alone, but an organized medium for gathering marine data.

In recent years, the methods and styles of marine angling have increased in number and in variety—as have the materials at the disposal of the angler. People have found (for instance) that brook-trout tackle will take many ocean fishes —and very excitingly. Black-bass gear (bait-casting tackle) takes even bigger and more violent fish than can be caught *anywhere,* in fresh water. Spinning does the same. There are other methods. The IGFA has been pressed to set up rules, standards and new world-record charts for all these and many allied types of "light-tackle" marine angling.

The subject has been exhaustively studied by officers and by interested member clubs (of which, at present, not many are concerned with ultra-light-tackle fishing). So far, no feasible system has been adopted for the fair, comparative appraisal of these many—often highly individualistic—styles of angling. Other associations and publications have made the effort and have failed, as did the IGFA. Acceptable "standards," even where so many methods are concerned, can be established,

166

but their administration is, so far as the IGFA can determine at this time, too complicated for practical, *world-wide* administration.

Goggle-fishermen (the men—and ladies—who dive beneath the waves with or without a sustaining "lung" to let them breathe under water), too, have petitioned the IGFA to set up a world-record chart for *them*. But their case, also, presented problems so far not adequately solved. For one thing, they do not catch fish by rod and reel at all—however "sporting" their manner of fish hunting may seem to be; for another, practically every goggle-fisherman has his own idea of what constitutes the right "weapon."

Hence—though the new *materials* for lines and rods have been tested, sent about to all member clubs for scrutiny and finally voted sporting (or not)—these innumerable and comparatively new ocean-fishing methods have not been included in what would be countless new panels of "records." The IGFA sticks to its old classifications, of which "twelve-pound test" (formerly "three-thread") line is the lightest—light enough line, surely, for any man who casts or lowers a bait in the ocean!

The cost of these many enterprises is defrayed by one man, to whom millions are indebted: Michael (or, as I've called him here, "Mike") Lerner. Pretty nearly everybody who knows him—and that includes potentates and porters in every segment of the round world's map—calls him Mike, anyhow. We might as well.

The Australian, Clive Firth, who suggested that we Americans should keep the records, assumed that fishing clubs would share the large cost. Mike decided otherwise. Already among the world's foremost big-game hunters, anglers—and a leading collector of museum specimens—Mike was a man in early middle life. In addition to his land-and-sea-roving, he had been one of the partners in the Lerner Stores (if that doesn't ring a bell in your head, ask your wife!), so he decided he owed a debt to his favorite sport of ocean fishing. Most men would have been satisfied with the fact that they'd contributed many huge specimens of fishes, and in some cases *whole rooms of specimens*, to a half dozen of the world's leading museums. Mike wasn't.

The IGFA, Mike decided, wasn't going to cost any angler a dime. It didn't—it doesn't—and he has made provision so that it probably never will. Mike didn't want the IGFA to be a "patriarchal" organization, however—a Mike-bossed affair. So it is the *member clubs* who make all the decisions on matters of principle and rules; on other matters, the committee decides. Among them, Mike has one vote, as do all the rest. Since the officers were picked for their experience, knowledge, reliability, tenacity and judgment, it can be suspected that Mike may be overruled. He sometimes is, since he is not piscatorially omniscient (and even though, if you, as an angler, were to have to pick a single judge of your fishing feats, you could not find a fairer or more thorough man, this side of Judgment Day!).

Many gentlemen of distinction, of means and good will cannot wholly resist turning a "foundation" or an "institution" set up by themselves into an instrument for collateral, personal publicity. The American public accepts that small vanity with tolerance—while it also gratefully accepts the vast benefits of numerous contributions to its weal. Mike didn't feel that way, either. Mike has no press agent. Nobody was ever hired to do "publicity" for the IGFA. The news it sends out (new records of a spectacular sort, word of rule changes or comment anent arguments amongst anglers) is dispatched by Miss LaMonte.

Being the founder of IGFA actually has meant a thousand times as much work as glory for Mike. He was asked—during the war, for example—to form a committee of experts to redesign the fishing gear for lifeboats and life rafts; he spent a long time in that important, tricky chore. The equipment his committee produced on Government request is standard, now, in all services. Mike then saw to it that a second "fishing kit"—a kit for fishing for *fun*—went out to servicemen who, in myriads, were spending the weary war months alongside some of the world's best fishing water—without even a hook or a line! Mike paid for the first several thousand of these "recreational fishing kits"; subsequently the Red Cross gave them away overseas. They were such a success that, finally, the Government took over their manufacture and distribution as part of its military program.

Mike also helped stage-manage an expedition (reported elsewhere in this volume) by which meat-hungry troops on lonely Ascension Island were taught to fish and so to furnish fresh meat for their table. He, and his redoubtable wife, Helen—who is, among women, as an angler and big-game hunter, what Mike is among men—were also asked by the Government, toward the end of the war, to make up a "show" of their movies and of samples of guns and rods, to tour overseas in hospitals and areas behind the front. The idea was to demonstrate what "super-sport" meant, to sports-loving American G.I.'s. So the Lerners became troopers—and their "tour" was a sensational success. It *should* have been! For they can answer almost any outdoor-sports query in the hunting-fishing field. And their movies—colored film of themselves actually hunting and fishing—are fascinating. At times, their pictures would satisfy the most thrill-crazed spectator alive—since, in these films, it is all-too-evident that to get a rifle shot or a film record or both at once, it often darn near cost a Mr. or a Mrs. Lerner!

Following the "law of human nature" I set down earlier, Mike finally went into the ultimate field: pure science. For the American Museum of Natural History he built, on the island of Bimini, a "field station" for research. There, in a magnificent laboratory, well-equipped, with a residence that comfortably houses as many as a dozen top research people at a time, scientists can study the twenty or more different ocean environments that meet at Bimini. Hundreds of individuals, dozens of institutions have now contributed to that center. Bookfuls of scientific papers are pouring from the laboratory. And it has become—owing partly to the value of primitive sea life for cell study and to its year-round availability—a cancer research center. Everything, from lab space to laundry, for every scientist who comes to the Lerner Marine Laboratory, is *free!* But that is another story—mentioned here merely to indicate that when a man starts fishing in the sea, what he finally "catches" will depend upon his imagination, his will and his personal capacity as much as upon his first bait or his final luck.

That's how the IGFA came into being. That's what it has led to, *so far!* Its worth to human relations the world over cannot be exaggerated. Its value as an umpire in a great sport is deeply appreciated by many and should be understood by all. Those who serve as its officers love fishing—and they love people, too. The boundless future of IGFA as a special instrument for gathering and sifting the unknowns of the sea gives it still another imposing facet.

An Australian dreamed it up. An American made it a fact, surpassing the dream. And *everybody* who wets a line in salt water—whatever his nationality, his bait or the fish he hopes to hang—has reason to rejoice in the result, the IGFA.

Some fishing

Listen to this tale of woe

Fishing is mostly tough luck. "The big ones get away" is its basic slogan. And the bigger a fish the angler seeks, the tougher his misfortune is likely to be. A universal belief that fishermen are philosophers is explained by that circumstance: they have to be. A man unable to take a philosophical attitude toward the tribulations of life certainly could not enjoy a sport in which immense patience is required, and a sport in which the reward for patience is often a titanic battle ending in utter defeat.

The calamities that may befall an angler who whips a

brook trout are fairly limited. He can, to be sure, fall into a deep pool and drown; he can step on a rattlesnake or in a hornet's nest; he can concentrate so hard on a fighting trout that he fails to evade a bull charging across a pasture. (Once in re this last problem, I was obliged to abandon fishing and dive over a barbed wire fence into a brook to escape a rushing bull.) But when a man takes himself out to sea with vastly heavier gear, he greatly increases the likelihood of misfortune even though he is reasonably safe from bulls, hornets, and serpents.

Consider, for example, an expedition made by me many years ago to the famed island of Bimini in the British West Indies. Fishing on the good ship *Neptune*, with Harold Schmitt, a redoubtable guide, I put in a solid week trying for blue marlin. A week becomes a long time, when you rise with the dawn and come back to shore at sunset, when the sea is a daylong, brazen glare of tropical sunshine and the brightwork on the boat becomes too hot to touch and when, after seven solid days, you haven't had a single bite! Under such conditions one is likely to grow restless and to reflect that one is spending a great deal of time (not to mention money!) doing exactly nothing in a fairly painful manner.

My mind was running in such a vein when, in the middle of the seventh afternoon, one of the big bonefish baits splashing along from an outrigger was hit suddenly and hard. "Barracuda!" Harold yelled from up on the canopy.

A man set for blue marlin is not interested in catching barracudas. They merely spoil baits, as a rule, without becoming hooked—for even a large 'cuda seldom grabs a whole, five-pound bonefish; he snatches perhaps half, cutting it in two.

I had rushed to the heavy rod when the fish splashed at the bait and set it in the gimbal of the fighting chair. I reeled in the bisected bait so we could put on another. But, as it came near the boat, the 'cuda swiped at it again. So I decided to try to catch the 'cuda as a kind of consolation for days of doing nothing at all. I threw the big reel on "free spool"—letting the line run out again. The bait drifted back and sank. That was to give the 'cuda plenty of time to pick up the last fragment of bonefish—which contained the hook.

When I thought I'd "dropped back" far enough for the 'cuda to devour the bait, I threw on the drag. There was, in this process, a period of about a *fifth of a second* in which I did not have a hand on the rod or reel and merely supported the tackle with my knee. One hand was resting on the free-spooling reel as a light brake, to prevent backlash. The other, very briefly, was used to snap on the brake or, as some anglers say, to put the reel "in gear."

During that fraction of a second, however, as I got the reel in gear, the line came tight. It tightened, in fact, with a violence and suddenness never before experienced by me. The heavy rod was yanked clear of my knee. I snatched at it and my fingers actually grazed it; a tenth of one second of additional time might have allowed me to get a grip on it. But there wasn't even that extra split instant. The rod leaped from the gimbal. The reel turned over in the air and whacked mightily against the transom in the stern. Then the rod and

177

reel bounced high and seemed to hang suspended in the sunshine for a moment before falling into the *Neptune's* foamy wake.

I was on my feet at once. I saw the tackle—eight hundred dollars' worth of it—settling in the cobalt Gulf Stream. I saw something else, presently. A tremendous blue marlin, deephooked, surged fifteen feet into the air not fifty feet astern! It made, in the ensuing moments, half-a-dozen sky-stabbing jumps in the attempt to shake my hook. Failing, it vanished, dragging behind it the eight hundred dollars' worth of tackle. That night I radiophoned to Miami for a new rod, reel and line.

Any marlin fisherman will understand what had happened, and how I had blundered. That marlin had been following my bait, deep down, out of sight, when the 'cuda cut in from the side and hit. Barracuda—and the invisible marlin—had then chased the mutilated bait together as I reeled in. When I dropped back, however, the *marlin*, not the 'cuda, took the bait. And, having seized it close to our stern, the marlin turned about and headed for parts unknown at full speed.

Just then, just *exactly* then, I'd slapped on the drag—and failed to keep a firm grip on the rod. I could have managed to hold it with my knee if the twenty or thirty pound 'cuda had been hooked. But the force of four or five hundred pounds of blue marlin taking off at perhaps thirty miles an hour relieved me of the tackle. We found, later, that the reel had hit the transom so hard it loosened twelve two-inch screws in mahogany!

Hard luck enough for one trip? Not at all! The very next

day, on a different rod (we were waiting for more marlin gear to come over by plane, that afternoon), I hooked a palpably big fish. Mrs. Wylie, who was fishing beside me, hooked one, also. We fought our "double header" (without knowing the identity of the quarry) for about a half hour before we began to see that, when her fish ran, mine did, and when I got line back from my fish, she got line; when her fish tore off in a new direction, mine took the same path. So we realized we had both hooked the same fish. That is a fairly common piscatorial hardship and an irritating one, since a catch made on two rods doesn't count as anybody's prize.

After perhaps an hour, we saw our fish—a big hammerhead shark. We weren't interested in catching shark. But we were interested in testing the steel rod which had been sent to me for that purpose by a tackle manufacturer. So my wife deliberately broke her line and I fished alone simply to see how much "pressure" the rod could stand. It stood a lot. Before long I was "working" on that shark with my drag screwed up tight, bending way back, like a man shoveling dirt over his head. I expected, of course, to break the line at some point in this experiment—for it was only fifteen-thread, with (in those days) a breaking strain of forty-five pounds.

But it was the rod that ultimately snapped. It snapped with a loud sound when bent almost double. And I felt a sharp pain in my left foot. The hollow steel shaft had broken in two in the middle. I still hung onto the butt. However, while so drastically bent, the rod had acted as a bow, the taut line as a bowstring, and the tip had broken off to become an arrow. The "arrow" was driven down into the top of my foot. It made a

179

circular cut, a cross-section of the rod, and only bone stopped the downthrust. Blood was flowing freely on the *Neptune's* deck and we put in for shore. To this day I bear a circular scar which looks as if it had been made by a miniature cooky cutter. The shark? In the excitement, or during the subsequent first aid, it got away.

End of bad luck? Not entirely. Two days later I "hung" another unidentified but very large fish and fought it all afternoon through squall-driven rain and past half a dozen roaring waterspouts. Night fell and new squalls appeared. The lights of Bimini were lost to view and we were obliged to break off the fish to avoid disaster—disaster in pitch-black, tempestuous seas which heaved around us and thundered frighteningly over near-by snaggle-toothed coral reefs. On that particular trip, in fact, we caught only a single fish. But, in all fairness, I should add that it was a white marlin, taken on light tackle, that it weighed ninety-nine pounds and is still the record in its tackle class for the Rod and Reel Club of Miami Beach.

Experiences of this sort ultimately started a train of thought in my mind. They seem unusual and some are. For instance, I do not know anybody else who's had a broken rod driven partway through his foot. But I saw my brother hurt himself badly (and lose a gigantic jewfish) when his rod broke and the force with which he'd been pulling drove the shattered butt against his forehead hard enough to cut it open. Had the break been an inch lower, he'd have lost an eye. But during the period when I was publicly belittling myself for losing a blue marlin owing to carelessness with a rod, Helen Lerner, one of the world's best big-game fisherwomen, told me that the identical accident had befallen her and that she, too, had contributed an expensive rod and reel to the briny deep. Furthermore, *her* rod had been sighted—rusted beyond use—a year later, in the reefs off Bimini. The hooked marlin had evidently swum through that area and the trailing tackle had caught in the coral, after which the fish had been able to free itself by pulling out all the line and breaking it.

In fact, whenever I told an angler of my misfortunes, I was told in turn of disasters similar, or greater, or funnier. There was, for example, a member of the above-mentioned club who, one day, went fly-fishing, in waders, on the "flats" of the Bay of Florida. He dragged in the water behind himself a gunny sack in which he put his fish, with a view to keeping them alive and thus fresh. The sack was tied around his waist so as to leave his hands free. In it, as he waded and cast his flies, he accumulated a nice mess of snappers, groupers, jack and so on.

He was quite surprised when the sack of fish trailing behind him suddenly pulled so hard it sat him down—in about twenty inches of wet ocean. He stood up and was pulled down again. That time, however, he perceived it was neither a miracle nor the combined effort of his caught fish which explained his embarrassment. A very large shark—a shark so big its dorsal fin and back stood well out of water—had taken the fish-filled gunny sack in its mouth. Understandably, though perhaps unwarrantedly, my fellow club member feared his little fishes might be regarded as mere hors d'oeuvres and that he might become the shark's main dish. He therefore untied the rope that attached the sack to his middle and abandoned his catch to the shark. During the time employed by the shark in ripping up the gunny sack, my friend made fast, splashy tracks for shore!

People who go fishing for large tarpon seem to be especially beset by misfortune. Only a few days ago, I read an account of two anglers who were engaged in a serious tarpon duel. It was at first "serious" merely owing to the fact that it involved a large wager on the biggest fish taken. The two competitors angled indecisively for some days and then, minutes apart, each hooked a whopper. One man was fishing in a rowboat; the other fished hard by in the stern of a cruiser.

The man in the small boat had battled his tarpon fairly close to defeat when the tarpon being fought by his colleague jumped aboard. In coming into the dinghy, the tarpon knocked down the embattled angler, damaged his rod and broke his line. Old angling hands would probably have called this "no contest" and continued the duel. But the two gentlemen in question took a different view. The man aboard the cruiser insisted that, even though his fish had jumped into the rowboat, it was "fair caught"—and he won the stakes. The man who was knocked down by it—though he'd lost his own hooked fish—insisted that, since the tarpon had pinwheeled aboard his craft, *he* had caught it! Newspaper accounts did not give the final decision on this subject—but it certainly constitutes hard luck of a most bizarre sort.

Hard luck! It's the litany of angling! One morning, off Miami, after many days of marlin trolling, a big "blue" rose behind my bait, followed it for a quarter of a mile, and then lunged, bill out, tail cutting the sea to foam. It was a sure strike, the start of a hard strike, a pretty fair bet that we'd hook him. And then, just as the marlin opened his mouth to gulp the bonefish, coming from nowhere a pelican dived with folded wings, beat the marlin by a foot, and flew off with the bait—until the line came tight and yanked it from the great bird's bill. The marlin, apparently overwhelmed with chagrin at so ignominious an event, made no effort to take a second bonefish we were trolling on the other outrigger. It departed. We saw no more marlin on that expedition.

Among tuna fishermen, a favorite tale of woe concerns the Cat Cay Tuna Tournament where, every year in the spring, some of the ablest and most obdurate deep-sea anglers in the world compete during the annual run of "horse mackerel." The huge fish swim north along the Bahamas' edge of the Gulf Stream in large schools, moving close to the surface. It is easy to sight them; it is often extremely difficult to present them with a bait which they will take. I have stood in the stern of a boat moving fast enough to keep just ahead of schools of four- and five-hundred-pounders, offering whole fish as bait and live fish, cut strips of fish, squid, feathers of various colors, and so on—and failed to get a single fish to turn from his group toward any lure.

In so hotly fought a contest as the Cat Cay tourney, a single fish may mean victory. Hence the moment when a tuna is distracted from a school and decides to take a bait is highly important—and tensely dramatic. One year, a contestant who for days had not been able to induce a tuna to hit finally got a fish to swing away from its migrating brethren. A strike, at long last, was virtually assured. Unfortunately, at that crucial moment, the mate—an intent young man—bent a little too far forward in the effort to view the exciting, smashing hit. He fell overboard directly in front of the fish. Not being a man-eater, the tuna scrammed. And the luckless angler lost his opportunity.

Long ago, as I've said, matters of this sort set me thinking. I had been made, by that time, a director of the corporation which manages the annual fishing tournament of the Miamis, Coral Gables, and surrounding suburbs and towns. This is said to be the biggest fishing derby in the world and, so far as I know, the claim has never been contested. After all, there are some six hundred species of fish in Florida waters, of which most are edible and many are game. These fish are, in general, abundant. And hundreds of thousands of people annually go in quest of them.

The prizes for the varied game species are valuable and there are several for each sort of fish, as the fishing method and the tackle used determine the classifications of winners. Some anglers fly-cast, some bait-cast, some use spinning gear and some troll with light lines or the heaviest lines obtainable. As the years had passed I had observed that, for every catch which won a prize, there were uncountable tales of disaster, ignominy and rugged misfortune.

So, a dozen years ago, I suggested to the tournament committee that these people, valiant even if unsuccessful, should also have a shot at a prize of some sort. There ought to be, I said, a consolation reward for the hapless man or woman or child who had, not the biggest fish, but, rather, the "toughest luck" of the whole tournament. The committeemen, being anglers, took a sympathetic view of the idea and, ever since, a silver cup has been awarded annually. It is called "the Philip Wylie Hard Luck Trophy" and I have never been certain that I liked the connection of my name with misfortune, though I will yield to few in the matter of bad breaks at fishing. This prize is, I believe, the only one of its kind in the world: not a "booby prize" but an award for grim effort in the face of hopeless predicament.

People amongst Miami's myriads of tournament entrants "compete" for the Hard Luck Trophy by the following method: if they believe their luck has been spectacularly bad, owing to circumstances surpassing the normal expectations of an informed piscatorial pessimist, they are invited to write out the details of their misfortune. At the end of the tournament, a board judges these accounts (which must be attested by others) and the cup is awarded. Needless to say, the trophy has elicited some somber tales.

For it is tough to win the "tough luck trophy." In fact, it is tough to try to decide, as a yearly judge, whose luck was foulest. For ordinary misfortune doesn't even count in such a contest. Every season, for instance, dozens or scores or perhaps hundreds of people, unused to the routine difficulties of deep-sea angling, enter a "hard luck" story without realizing it is a "normal" trial, to the old hand.

Thus, in 1941, the first year of the contest, the cup did not go to applicant R. A. Langley of Milton, Massachusetts. He hung what he at first assumed was the bottom of the sea. But it moved. In fact, it fought so tirelessly and so savagely that his companions in the cruiser began to ask for transportation else-

185

where, before the unknown monster should be boated. The fish finally showed—a tiger shark, "estimated" at fifteen hundred pounds and "guaranteed" to go over a thousand. Mr. Langley didn't catch the shark; it finally straightened out his heavy steel hook as if it had been a bent pin—and escaped. But straightened hooks are not regarded by old hands as particular misfortunes—any more than "frozen reels."

Many an angler—including your correspondent—has lost a fish that would have been a world record because, during the battle, the ceaseless in-and-out running of line under tension gradually spreads apart the flanges of a reel until they jam —or "freeze"—against the sides. There is no way, after that, to give or take in line—and the angler almost invariably loses a fish which then makes an easy lunge against a line that doesn't give—breaking it.

The final contest for the Hard Luck Trophy, that first year (if memory serves me correctly), was between Mr. Joe Nieser's "hundred-dollar dinner" and Mr. Jim Scully's "two-hour world record."

Mr. Nieser, while fishing from the Venetian Causeway (which connects Miami and Miami Beach) caught a six-pound pompano on very light tackle. An old fishing hand, well aware that the catch was excellent for the gear used, Mr. Nieser carefully weighed his prize on the scales in his tackle box. Then he hurried home. Three guests were due for dinner. In view of the fact that fresh pompano is among the greatest of delicacies, the fish was cut in fillets, served, and eaten. During the meal, Mr. Nieser choked. His pompano had not been weighed *officially* and according to the rules. He rushed to the phone. Sure enough, it would have been an *all-time* tournament record. But it was not even eligible—it was digesting. H. H. Hyman, chairman of the committee, calculated later, for the benefit of the anguished Mr. Nieser, that his prize would have been worth more than a hundred dollars, hence the meal had cost the angler twenty dollars a portion—as well as a tournament record. "Pompano," Mr. Hyman said, "is, to be sure, an expensive delicacy—but twenty bucks a portion is on the high side."

Mr. Nieser applied for the Hard Luck Cup. So did a famed and skillful angler named Jim Scully, whom I happen to know. Jim longed above all things to have his name inscribed on the IGFA world-record rolls. And one afternoon while fishing over the reefs off Florida, he took a fifty-three-pound amberjack on "4-6" tackle—gear hardly heavier than that used by black-bass fishermen in fresh water. Jim kept the IGFA record charts in his tackle box. He scanned them. Sure enough, his catch qualified as a world record! He was being cheered and toasted by his companions on board the fishing cruiser when one of them, a Mr. Bert Harborn, also using "4-6" tackle, hooked another amberjack. It had taken Jim two hours to whip his fish on such light gear; Bert took about as long, only—and it was an important only—his fish weighed fifty-eight and a half pounds. So Jim's name was not inscribed on the rolls of fame. The unprecedented thing had happened: a world record had fallen twice, on the same day, from the same boat. The tournament committee decided that Mr. Nieser had been a shade negligent in the matter of the pompano. But Jim had suffered a pure brand of that hard luck which dogs all fishermen.

Some fishing

The next year, Sam Holden of Ottawa, Canada, was the chief contender. Mr. Holden hired a charterboat and fared forth innocently to fish. Somewhere off the alabaster skyline of Miami he hung, battled and boated a white marlin which he brought in with *élan*, weighed and hung on the fish rack for all to see. It weighed one hundred and thirty pounds. It was bigger than any tournament winner in the previous several years and looked to be a sure first. Word got around on the following morning, however, that Mr. Holden's marlin was ineligible because it had been "mutilated by a shark." Judges rushed to the scene and, sure enough, a pound or so of marlin had been devoured—by what proved to be a stray cat roaming the docks during the night! Mr. Holden's relief was soon dashed. For he found he had caught the marlin on a charterboat that was not eligible to compete in the tournament. So his fish was ruled out. But it *was* eligible for a different, currently running competition, the George Ruppert Fishing Contest—with a two-hundred-and-fifty-dollar first prize.

This litany of disaster has continued down years crowded with unspeakable misfortune. For example:

There is the case of Ernie Woolfe, a noted angler and a Miami Beach realtor. He took a ten-pound bonita on spinning gear, one day—weighed it and measured it and sent for judges to inspect it and denote it as what it was: a record. Before they arrived (and while Ernie was phoning proudly to his folks), a mate—new to the business—cut the prize up for strip baits! *No* record.

A recent winner of my Hard Luck Trophy didn't catch a fish at all. His name is Norman Theriot. During the 1950 tournament he had found and staked out a spot where some especially large barracuda and crevallé jack hung out. On the last day of the tournament, with very light tackle, Norman, in a skiff, went out to do what he was sure he could: break the records in a class or two. He made one cast, got one enormous strike—and then—because it was a windy morning—in the sea nearby a skiff overturned, and one of its three occupants was drowned immediately. Norman, by a Homeric feat of swimming, of wading in seas that surged over him, of running his own small skiff in surf, rescued the other two, resuscitated them, and finally got aid for them on the lonely beach where he'd brought them ashore. He didn't get a record, he didn't even get a chance to fish, but he did get the Hard Luck Cup—and the Carnegie Medal!

There was a man who claimed the cup (but wasn't awarded it) because, just as he was about to get a hit from "the biggest sailfish the captain had even seen" (this, by the way, is a classical description of lost fish), his wife's hat blew off, hit the fish on the bill, was impaled, and frightened the fish away.

Another worthy, fishing on a drawbridge, hung one of those "lost monsters" and fought it for half an hour. Then a bell rang and the drawbridge started up. The man jumped to terra firma and continued his struggle. However, owing to the position of the fish, the river and the canted bridge, his line now sawed back and forth across a lamp post. Finally it was frayed in two—and the fish escaped.

In the record is another yet more somber tale. An angler caught a world-record tarpon while fly-fishing from the bank of

189

some nameless Florida estuary. He slew the fish, weighed it on his own scales, noted it went several pounds over the current record, and set it in the shade while he continued his sport. When the sun sank, he went back to the spot to retrieve his prize—and found its tail vanishing between the jaws of a large alligator!

Lines that lead from busy anglers to desperate fish and run out for three or four hundred yards are often cut by the prows of majestic freighters which plow south along the golden sands of Miami's shore, just inside the north-racing Gulf Stream. But one of the saddest stories I ever heard concerned a nameless Keys gladiator who was casting in the old days from a trestle on the railroad line that once ran to Key West. Inadvertently, he let his back-cast dribble into the sea. It was thereupon seized by a big tarpon. He whirled about to give battle—and stepped back quickly. A Florida East Coast train was bearing down, whistling. The gentleman's line was parted by its locomotive!

Then I recall the case of the fellow who went fishing and was *himself* caught. There were three men in the skiff—plug casting. One of them, Tom Dupree, a Miami pioneer and realtor (real estate men seem to get mixed up often in these events), gave a mighty swing and planted all three of the triple-hook gangs on his plug in the scalp of a companion. The leader was cut. It was seen that a long trip back to the cruiser and a certain amount of minor surgery by another member of the party (who, luckily, was a doctor) would be required. But the thrice-hooked angler insisted that the blow had deadened his nerves and that he felt no pain. So he went on fishing the rest of the afternoon—and won all the bets of that day. Mr. Dupree insists the man won all wagers, owing to the fact that the plug, dangling from his skull, "flashing like a Christmas Tree ball—and jingling with every cast," unnerved everybody else and spoiled their skills. Possibly so. Anyhow, it didn't hurt. I should know—I was the guy caught.

Then, there's the true story of the woman who was pulled overboard by a strike: tackle, harness, wicker chair and all; if she hadn't been a good swimmer——

But I forbear.

Fishing, as I said at the start, is mostly hard luck. But it's a wonderful sport—why dwell on its hazards? I'm going fishing, myself, in the Keys, this week. Maybe I'll——

What makes a great day's fishing?

The angler has one advantage over other sportsmen: he doesn't mind growing old, nearly as much. The hunter, when his limbs tire with the years, has to narrow his range, to give up, perhaps, the hunt itself and, at long last, to shoot clay pigeons from a wheelchair. The fancy diver, the skier, the vigorous horseman are, as a rule, forced by age to lessen their activities; even tennis players must slow down; golfers play fewer holes—and those less strenuously. Age early retires most professional athletes. But the angler, whose principal act is patient sitting, can—if necessary—simply reduce the heft of his quarry and the size of his tackle so that, even as an old and feeble man, he can get from a bass or a ladyfish, with a trout or spinning rod, the same relative challenge, comparable thrills.

The world is full of very old men—and women—who fish; it contains few who climb dangerous mountains. So when a certain magazine editor asked me to write of the highlights of my own fishing, it came with something of a shock that I had fished (already!) for forty years, and a bit more. I next remembered the essay F. Scott Fitzgerald wrote on becoming forty years old; he felt, at that age, the glamour and excitement of life had ended and everything ahead was dull stuff. I could not help wondering how he would have felt if he had been an angler—a real one. For then he would have had an area of interest where age was not a measure; he might easily have reasoned from that fact to a happier philosophy.

Maybe this is the reason fishermen are so universally regarded as philosophical men: not their patience—which is commonly given as the explanation—but the fact that they are unworried by any prospect of abandoning their pursuit. They have a special bond with Nature—one that makes them as if ageless and unaging—which gives a special peace and perspective.

Fishing is patience. It is also high excitement. But its highest moments are not always made up of the "big one that *didn't* get away." Often that's it—to be sure. But sometimes, the big one that *did* get away provides a more memorable experience than the one that broke a record. Frequently, too, it is the *other fellow's* catch which makes a landmark in the recollection. And sometimes it is not the fish at all but a person met on a riverbank or at some salty dock—or it is a landscape, a seascape, or the mood of both.

I have fought and caught very big fish in whistling weather, far at sea, with green water coming aboard the boat and things breaking, things tumbling, mate and skipper falling on the sluicing deck, and night cracking down to add to our common ardors. Such adventures take a certain amount of stamina and even, perhaps, a trifle of *sang froid,* a touch of what, in less-classical words, is called "ice water in the veins." I am not a particularly brave man; yet, like many others of sometimes flagging nerve, I have managed to get myself into several spots which, afterwards, gave me alternately a sense of bravura and sweaty moments in the late night when I remembered—and couldn't get myself to sleep.

Yet, for all of that, and for sheer excitement, I think I had the most from the first big fish I ever caught. It weighed four pounds and a quarter. It was a smallmouth black bass.

All one July, with half a dozen other kids my age—which was twelve—I'd tried to catch one of the large bass we could clearly see from the banks of a private lake. Four- and five-pounders, they appeared frequently in the late afternoon, in the green shade of a stand of lofty white pines. We kids found them there early in the month. We set about at once, of course, to try to catch them on such random rods, reels, lines and hooks as small boys assemble; and we did not try sporty bait —artificial flies, plugs, spoons, or the like.

We used grasshoppers, worms, frogs. The mildly interested bass—sometimes a dozen were in view at once—would come up from their idle coursing in the verdant depths to inspect our offerings. And to turn away. But we soon found that if we threw in a grasshopper or live frog *unattached* to our gear, the wily fish would rise less suspiciously, take a good look, and engulf the prey—often with a soul-satisfying smash of the calm lake surface. However, we *never* hooked one, though various members of our barefooted, eager-beaver company bought, begged and stole gut leaders of the most transparent sort. Every ruse failed.

And then my great day came.

I took a rowboat out alone and anchored one sunny mid-morning in a deep place in that pond. As bait that day I'd been able to provide myself with nothing better than a few bluegill minnows, hand-seined from along the banks. (We had preferred "shiners" and dace.) For some reason—the failure of all other means, no doubt—I decided to put a small split shot on my line and let my minnow ride down to the muddy bottom fifteen or twenty feet below. And I sat there a long while, not very expectantly. When my strike came, it was an easy thing. I imagined a bullhead or bluegill had taken my small minnow. But when I hit back to set the hook, things changed.

The bass took off deep. He tried several runs down there and I burned my fingers on a cheap reel that had a click but no drag. (I didn't know about the burns until later.) Then the bass rose and jumped and I could see with my own naked, popping eye I'd hooked one of the lunkers we'd sought for so long. I suppose it took ten or fifteen minutes to fight the fish to the boatside. I daresay no subsequent and equal period of

my life has ever put me under greater emotional strain or produced more pure excitement. And I got him. With the quench-
less optimism of small boys we—all of us—carried landing nets
when we went forth to fish. It was the first time I'd ever used
one on anything but perch and small pickerel.

I heaved him aboard, upped anchor, rowed ashore like
a demon and paraded through the summer cottages with sensational effect. He was proudly photographed by a dozen adults
including two college men. He was, that night, proudly eaten
by my family and myself. And to this day, every detail of that
lake is fixed in my mind; I can still taste its sweet muddiness
and smell the wind from the pines coming across it and see the
brilliance of the sun on its cat-pawed surface.

Here, however, the story takes a shameful turn. I was
twelve and I was the only boy in the community who'd caught
a black bass, let alone a four-and-a-quarter-pounder. If I had
been a sportsman in the grownup sense of the word, I would,
of course, have immediately told all the rest of my "gang"
where and with what I'd caught the colossus. Unfortunately
for this record, my thoughts took a different twist. I was not in
the least eager to have some other kid take a bass as big or
perhaps even bigger. I felt sure I'd found the "secret" of how
to catch those wise lunkers. So, when I was importuned for the
piscatorial details, I finally—and with apparent reluctance—
told the other boys I'd caught that bass on *jelly*.

"You know," I said, "we *never* got them to bite a frog or
minnow or locust or anything on a hook. So I swiped a jar of
jelly—good, firm *apple* jelly—and I put a gob on my hook and
tossed it out and before it sank, even—*whamo!*"

197

Some fishing

All the rest of the summer, through August and until the schoolbell rang again, the lake was dotted with rowboats in which small boys—and some girls—were feverishly trying to get *jelly,* swiped from their mothers' jam closets, to stay on a hook! Just as I'd figured, it didn't. And the bass didn't seem to care for it, anyhow. But, at the same time, I was out there, too, nearly every day, in a boat of my own—with jelly of my own, of course, as a ruse—and some further bluegill minnows, caught furtively. And it is only fair to report that even though I used gross treachery to aid me, I never did get another bass bite that year.

A time comes in the lives of most youths when they *make things.* They send away for parts and diagrams and assemble airplanes. They buy blocks of straight-grained white pine, fix them in vices in their cellars and, with drawknives and chisels, painstakingly begin to shape the hulls of model ships. Or they go, as I did for a while, from one drugstore to another—buying (with a different alibi for each purchase) such substances as sulphur, charcoal, potassium nitrate—or chlorate—and the like. The object of that is homemade gunpowder.

A time came for me when I read a book on how to split bamboo, shape it, glue the segments together and make a fly rod—and how to tie flies, too. The rods I made, I realize now, were absurdly clumsy things—the guides wound on imperfectly—and the reels fitting poorly. The flies I tied were composed mostly of substitute materials: I couldn't come by buck tails or grouse feathers, offhand. They looked like no standard trout fly and certainly like no living insect, in spite of the variety in that vast kingdom.

198

Nevertheless, I fared forth with this ungainly equipment (and much information about how to cast) and I fished many times in streams and millponds that *looked* "fishy" to me. I lost most of my homemade flies in trees and high bushes and on logs too far offshore to reach. But at long last, one afternoon, a trout—a genuine brook trout, a good inch over the legal length, a trout that was perhaps starving to death or possibly astigmatic or myopic—took my fly and I took him.

Nobody—repeat—*nobody* ever brought a marlin to dock with greater satisfaction than I felt then. For who that goes in search of marlin makes his own rods and fashions his own baits artificially? Who does it alone and unaided from start to finish? Who does it from a book and without any guide *but* that? What a victory—that seven-inch trout! I cannot recall, exactly, the first sailfish I ever hooked and fought and brought to boat. But I shall not forget that trout—ever.

There is a satisfaction in catching giant fish, too.

My first whopper was a tuna and the day I caught him I'd invited a girl to go along. We set out from Brielle, New Jersey, on a hot morning and went clear to Ambrose Light before anchoring and starting to chum. Hours passed. The wind came up from the southwest. The anchored cruiser began to pitch. And its skipper, who was as "green" as I (in the sense that he'd never taken one of the great game fish aboard his boat), began to worry about the weather.

Then, suddenly, the heaving sea around us showed the telltale whirlpools and "boils" sent up by the tails of tuna. Soon we saw huge glimmerings of them in the murky water. Tensely we waited and presently our coil of line on the gunwale began to slip rapidly into the sea: a tuna had taken our bait. I leaped into the fighting chair and struck when the slack line had payed out. The reel screamed and its oil smoked. The skipper cast loose the anchor on a flagged buoy (that slowly and forever sank as we tore away)and the fight began.

It is quite a shock, even after sailfish and amberjack, and sharks, to tangle with a tuna or a marlin or some other fish of that ilk. For quite a while I felt as if, in a horrid nightmare, I'd taken on Jack Dempsey for a grudge-fight. Every time the tuna raced away I felt the pressure would pull me apart. Every time he slackened his assault and I horsed him rhythmically back to a point some hundreds of yards from the boat, I felt that I could not possibly do it again. But that was all in the *first* hour. (Besides, you will remember, I had that girl on board; she was an important girl—she is Mrs. Wylie now—and, after all, I'd told her I was something of a fisherman.) The second hour was, surprisingly, less alarming and painful. I had "settled down." I had my second wind. And I even got through the third hour in reasonable condition.

But, by the time the fourth hour began, the wind was blowing a good thirty knots and the sea was heavy. We were miles up the Lower Bay from the region of the Lightship, where we'd hung the fish. The afternoon was waning. Nevertheless, the skipper remained dauntless (he'd been a "wooden ship" sailor in the "iron men" days—as he often reminded what he considered wooden types of charterboatmen) and I hung on because there was, in the lexicon of sports fishing, nothing else to do. I did not even know, then, how to "use" a heavy sea to help in the taking of a heavy fish—the way to

200

employ the rise and fall of the boat itself as a substitute for back-breaking effort, getting in line from the lift of the waves instead of the personal lift of one very weary P. Wylie. But I panted on and the tuna finally turned almost belly up and I heaved him alongside.

The bruising adventure was ended, I thought; actually, it hadn't begun. Our skipper had rigged a derrick for "boating" monstrous fish. It was his own idea. This was now lowered: a "V"-shaped boom—and the tuna was gaffed. The gaff-rope led over a pulley at the apex of the boom and from that point to a block-and-tackle. Captain, mate and girl manned the lines and—sure enough—five-hundred-odd pounds of tuna came up and out of the raging sea. The derrick was so designed that, once the fish had been elevated to a sufficient height, the boom could then be raised by a second block-and-fall, bringing any sea giant neatly aboard.

But the ingenious captain had not figured on the strain of a horse mackerel at the end of his tubular steel supports. And he had not figured on a heavy sea. The great fish hung out there in the air, astern, against the fading sunset, swinging in tremendous arcs as the boat rolled and pitched. Now it swept far away—and now in toward us so that all hands had to duck the whishing passage of its tail. Then, suddenly, both bolts which anchored the derrick sheared. Like power-driven lances, the great steel rods tore into the cabin, splitting out pieces of its wooden sides and smashing its windows, in a crash and roar of glass which was, luckily, thrown outward on both sides. And luckily—very luckily—nobody happened to be in the path of the back-rammed steel. Nobody was hurt and only the superstructure of the cruiser suffered: it looked as if it had taken a burst of small cannon shells.

The tuna went back in the sea, of course. And the gaff came out. Furthermore, in spite of its minutes of prodigious dangling, it was alive, still. It swam. But the hook hadn't been removed and I grabbed the rod once more. Once again I brought the tuna back to the boatside and this time, with ropes and backs and no derrick, skipper, mate and I brought the fish aboard. Darkness was falling then.

We headed home, quartering the wind the long way to Brielle, without any glass to protect us from the surging seas and without any dinner. We didn't make port until after midnight and I shall never know why we didn't go on the rocks at the difficult Manasquan inlet: small-craft warning had long since been sent out. Perhaps it was true about the skipper and iron men. Anyway, he brought in safely his half-wrecked boat, the girl, his mate and me and my first really big-game fish. I must report here, in all honesty, that the next morning I had to have help to get out of bed. I do not know how many thousands of muscles the anatomists have located and named; but I do know every one of them, on me, that day, was not just stiff and sore but nearly paralyzed and in a state of excruciation. For two days afterward, bellhops had to help me get dressed.

The girl who witnessed this exploit may have been led (falsely) to imagine me as a man of immense character and stubbornness. As Mrs. Wylie, she has learned since (if such was the case) that my character falls short of that degree of virtue in many areas. But, in the matter of *fishing*, I have thus far done all I could to hang on to every one I hooked, with a single exception. That principle is pretty absolute—in fishing. (Though, before I went after big tunas again, I made sure I was in better "condition" than I'd been on my first day.)

The exception? When would an angler—a proud man—*give up* on a fish? I did it once, off Bimini, years later. We'd hung—one hot, still afternoon—what we believed to be a blue marlin, on a special outfit that held a thousand yards of nine-thread line. Nobody, in those days, had "taken" a blue marlin on nine-thread.

The fish went down and the afternoon hours passed. Squalls came up from across the Bahama Flats. Lightning cracked all around us in the turbulent sea and lightning flew amongst the black clouds. Cold winds blew intermittently and brought tumults of stinging rain—hurtful, hard rain in which I had to stand, fighting the deep-down fish on my light tackle. Clear, sunny hours passed too, when I was hot and sweated hard and the mate poured buckets of sea water over me. Waterspouts drove by—sometimes too close for comfort. Night fell and the weather closed in. We began to lose sight, from time to time, of Bimini's faint lights. And with the prospect of being lost out there all night, in foul weather, the skipper asked me to bring the fish up or break him off. In trying to do the former, I broke him off—and we went home fishless for dinner.

That was the only time I ever broke one off deliberately. And it was the nearest I've ever come to boating a blue marlin on nine-thread line. I wasn't very near for, if it *was* a marlin (and we were never sure, since no one saw the strike and the

fish never jumped), I was doubtless a long way from success—
for it might have been a five- or six-hundred-pounder, probably an impossible catch for such tackle even under perfect
conditions.

Still, *I remember that unsuccessful afternoon* as vividly
as the equally uncomfortable one on which I got the tuna.
Why? Because, I think, the best part of angling is the *chance*.
It is the gamble. It is not *catching* fish that matters most, but
being occupied with fishing. For those who take their excitement from betting on horses, the principal thing is not to win
—who ever got rich at that?—but *to be at the track,* to see the
ponies run, to try to pick a winner-at-long-odds. In the aggregate, over the years, the bettors lose. Once in a while,
they do make big strikes—and get the biggest of the thrills they
seek. But they are *satisfied* to be at the races—win, lose or
draw; and so it is with angling.

So it is, I should say, except on *special* occasions. To be
sure, any beginner in quest of any particular fish will yearn to
get a hit from it, tangle with it and net it, boat it or haul it
ashore. But the maturing angler will gradually lose that avid-
ity: *fishing*, not fish-*catching* will become the greater part of
glamour for him. But, as I say, there are exceptions. For instance, any normal man, taking out for his first time a close
friend, will revert to his own first overeagerness and avidly
implore Triton, Neptune, Poseidon or some other Fish-God for
luck—for his friend. And once in a while you are put on your
mettle. As a rule, that's bad.

I recall a time (I'm sure "security regulations" do not
hold here, any longer) early in the Second World War when

I had the custom of taking fishing on a charterboat, on alternate Sundays, enlisted men, and then officers—who happened to be on duty at the local Naval Air Station. The commanding officer was a very good friend of mine and a gentleman much admired by me. He—or perhaps his WAVE—made up the regular Sunday list of four who would accompany me. But one Sunday I was sent a "ringer"—a man the C.O. phoned was a "doggone civilian" but a "close friend" whom he "hoped I'd take out," as "the guy loved fishing."

Of course, I accepted the civilian. He proved to be a rather short but very sturdy-looking bird of middle age, with a reddish face and a pair of the most penetrating eyes I've ever tried to penetrate back. He wore slacks and a woolen shirt and an old mackintosh—and he was accompanied by a brace of very respectful lieutenant commanders, both wearing wings, both—I happened to know—hot pilots and superior training officers at the base. The situation perplexed me until introductions were made and I heard my guest's British accent. Civilian he might be; VIP he surely was; and there was something indomitable about him, something Churchillian.

Out we went—on Harold Schmitt's *Neptune*. It was winter and I have never seen a lousier winter day off Miami. The wind picked up in the morning from twenty-five to about forty. It was gray and cold. Low clouds scudded over a jagged, pitted, nasty sea with swells a good thirty or forty feet high, long troughs and a cross-chop that threw the *Neptune* around like a toy boat in a cement mixer. The civilian—Mr. "Something" he had muttered—watched eagerly while the boat took the formidable smashing at the exit from Government Cut. He

205

fairly licked his lips when the careening mate put out baits. He selected a fishing chair and sat down in it just about the way the Rock of Gibraltar must have come to rest at the west end of the Mediterranean.

Meantime, the two lieutenant commanders also took chairs and held rods. Both these gentlemen were, as I said, distinguished fliers. Both were stunt pilots and both had acted as test pilots. Both later distinguished themselves beyond all mortal praise in the war—which, then, had not yet been poured hot and wicked on U.S.A. One had been a football player and the other a boxer, at the Academy. They were both experienced men on battleships, aircraft carriers and even, in one case, on destroyers.

But nobody had told them that there is something different about a thirty-eight-foot boat in a sea piled by a forty-knot wind and turned vile for the steadiest mariner by a cross-chop. Nobody, in other words, had explained that any man who claims to have *fished* in a number of oceans, in all weathers, over many years—without ever feeling a touch, *at least* of slavering, green-jowled *mal de mer* is a liar. I'll go further: a *damned* liar. And I'd go *still* further, if editors weren't so sparing of your manners.

Maybe I should add that these two American officers wore the gold-braid loops of special "aides." It suggested, strongly, that my British "civilian" was not exactly that. At any rate, as time passed, as the cold wind whistled, as rain fell in sullen spittings, as the outriggers whistled and the *Neptune* rode high, dropped low with elevator speed—and slewed and rolled in a thousand unexpectable ways, the two airmen slowly turned the warning saffron color that shows the onset of seasickness. Then, after a visible, long and very grim struggle, they began to show the greenish hue that betokens the more advanced stages.

All that time, the Britisher trolled like part of the ship, his eyes bright as jewels and fixed on the bait, his cheeks as rubicund as apples. "Great day!" he said once. "Active! Should bring the fish up!"

More time passed and I began to offer up sympathetic prayers for the pilots. After all, they were my countrymen. After all (I wagered myself), they could take up the Englishman in one of their fighters and make him as sick and frightened as a cat in a churn.

I was wrong.

When we'd stood about three hours of heaving, teetering, smacking down like a sledge from some wave-pinnacle and generally batting the *Neptune* into a full demonstration of her ruggedness, and yet no fish appeared, the Englishman began to ask questions. He asked them of me. He wanted to know how well acquainted I was with the Commanding Officer of the Naval Station. He wanted to know my views on the war and England. It happened I knew some Britishers he knew; it happened, too, that I had already been "tapped" by our Government for a certain job in the event of anything like— Pearl Harbor. Thus reassured, the gentleman abruptly confessed that he was an admiral in the British Navy.

And not just *any* admiral—but one whose name everybody knew. And not just a so-called "battleship" admiral, for he had commanded an aircraft carrier. And not just that, but, if he'd been in uniform, he would have had such wings as my American colleagues had. He would *also* have seen combat in the air! And, finally, he was famed for thinking out and pulling off what was, at the time, the greatest single-carrier air raid in history. It had cost one of England's two main enemies the bulk of their sea power. The admiral told me all these things in detail—confidentially, of course—and he told me something of the nature of his current mission in U.S.A.

I could see that the lieutenant commanders were distressed at these "violations" of security. Indeed, later, when I was an "accredited" war correspondent for the Navy, they told me so. (Though in fact it was up to the admiral to decide what to say or what not to say to me.) Their distress at the admiral's seeming "indiscretion" (I have always like to think, since then, that he was merely a gifted narrator and a good judge of people who could and would keep their mouths shut—though, possibly, the C.O. had told him I could be trusted) had a further bad effect on the officers. Both lieutenant commanders had barely been holding their own. Shock at the fact that the admiral was telling me the whole inside story of British naval strategy and giving me supersecret war information prevented them from holding on any further. They went to the gunwales, astern. Sadly and in vast humiliation, they became ill. And they *stayed* ill. By and by, they knelt on the decks and clung to the gunwales, unmindful of sluicing scuppers; it was convenient for them to be there, all the time.

The admiral gave them no more than a vaguely interested glance—and went on with his story. The point of part of it was particularly interesting—to me: the admiral, all his life, had been *a sports fisherman.* Not in naval regalia but as a plain "Mr. So-and-so," he had fished in and around most ports of the world, in most harbors and most other relevant waters. While fishing, he had made close note of naval matters, in every case.

The main case happened to involve a harbor where, for many years, a fleet base was built up by one of the nations then at war with Great Britain. The harbor and the sea outside offered tuna fishing. So on a number of different years, the slightly disguised admiral had tuna-fished there. In the course of doing that, he had also noted the warships and ways, piers, docks, channels, berths, mooring places and other details bearing on the nation's battle fleet. So, when war came, the admiral had been able to plan *precisely* how so many planes of such-and-such types, striking in succession, with such-and-such weapons, could "old boy, really mangle that base!"

He—and his carrier—her men—her planes and their pilots, bombardiers and gunners—had truly "mangled" the main enemy fleet, some weeks before—as all the world knew. What the world didn't know was *how.* And that was the fact—one set of facts—given me that rugged day. Needless to say, I was fascinated. Needless to say, I never mentioned the tale till the war was won. Because he talked in what my fellow-Americans deemed an "out-of-turn" way to me—an American, not Navy-connected—I have still kept his name in the dark. Naval historians, however, if any happen to read the above, will know who the angler and genius was, what port his aircraft struck, and that his single strike took the sting from the main naval arsenal of Mussolini.

Some fishing

I've told you that fishermen were philosophers; I should have said quite a lot of them were darned smart, too. They have to be, to catch some kinds of fish!

However—absorbing although I found the admiral's confidences that day—I was *host;* and the other two of my "guests" were getting mighty sick. Still, the admiral didn't suggest going in. That's the maritime tradition.

Harold Schmitt, my boatman-skipper and guide, several times whispered that we ought to take in those "poor devils." And he agreed emphatically with my opinion that we were not going to get a fish that day. It was too cold. We were the only boat out—but a thousand wouldn't have had a strike in such weather. Yet the admiral, hanging on, made me tell Harold to hope and pray for one fish, at least—which we could use as an excuse for abandoning a sea unfit for fish, let alone cruisers.

There was—I must confess—another factor. *I was sick,* too. I've been sick at sea perhaps five times in many, many hundreds of trips. But that day, with the sight of two pilots dog-sick, with a host's anxiety to take them inside where it was calm, with my embarrassment over their distress caused by the unfolding of a highly secret military narrative—or maybe just because it was so damned rough!—I got it. I made up my mind, though, that if I *split,* there was going to be one American on that boat besides mate and guide who didn't show any signs of *mal de mer* to the British hero.

Occasionally all of us perform small deeds of private, invisible, unknown bravery that, as we know, will never be adequately appreciated. If, ever, I should perform some reward-worthy and spectacular act of heroism (which possibility I doubt), I'm going to want a medal *not for that* but for the day I sat on the deck beside that admiral, six careening hours, and by main force of will and national pride *didn't* snap my cookies.

In midafternoon, by the grace of the angered sea gods, the *Neptune* took an especially big one, teetered, and came down like a house pushed off from a bridge. The smack all but knocked out our teeth. And it split three planks in that sturdy vessel. We began to take more water than we could pump. There wasn't any sane way to make repairs at sea. And even the admiral agreed we'd better high-tail for calm water, if not shore itself. Maybe he was a bum swimmer. Anyhow, you never saw two more relieved naval officers or one more grateful writer.

That was one day when I desperately wanted fish—a fish anyhow, for the Englishman. And we got none whatsoever. We went in to calm water and fished for pan fish a while and ate a little food. The admiral basked contentedly and the pilots recovered (and so did I) but we didn't get even a grunt or a sand perch.

Sometimes it goes the other way.

I've written a lot of fishing stories as well as four books which are collections of published and unpublished fishing yarns. (Readers who *don't* know that last can regard the statement as an advertisement.) Anyhow, the next account concerns the descent upon me in my south Florida home of a VIP, a northern editor, who had been responsible for the publication of many of my narratives and essays. Let us call him Mr. Smith.

It began with a "Dear Phil" letter from the said Mr.

Some fishing

Smith. "I will be in Miami," he said, "with my wife and son, over the entire day of the twelfth of next month. We'll arrive on the eleventh and hope you and your wife and daughter will be our guests for dinner. It's our hope that, on the twelfth, you'll be able to arrange a day of fishing for us, as I want to find out about these lavish accounts of Gulf Stream angling which you produce for us." It went on in that somewhat ironical vein. The above isn't verbatim—but it's a close approximation. A postscript added, "My wife and son—he's twelve—don't fish much and all I've ever caught is a few bullheads in Middle Western rivers."

You now get the idea:

He and his wife—a comely and reasonable woman—with his son—an alert and good-looking young character—were giving yours truly *one day,* one short, *arbitrary day,* to "prove" all I've written about Gulf Stream angling. That includes the high spots of my own twenty years of it—and the peaks and dramatic valleys in the angling careers of hundreds of people known to me, heard of by me, and purely fictitious, too. Gulf Stream fishing is unpredictable, like all other fishing. If the urgent Mr. Smith had said he was going to be in Miami for a month and asked me to take out himself and family on three or four hand-picked days, days when the fishing was known to be "hot," I'd have felt the proposition was hopeful.

As it was, I didn't. Who would, knowing the odds? Nevertheless, I chartered a fine boat, well ahead. I briefed up its skipper and mate for the big event. We were going to try everything short of dynamite to get fish, when the Smiths went down to sea in our ship.

What makes a great day's fishing?

The month turned. Fishing fell off. In the days preceding the twelfth, not only did the sailfish apparently vanish from our area but all other fish besides—even the reef fish—so that, from the fifth to the twelfth, boats by the score came into Miami's docks with no fish at all, or perhaps only one or two pickerel-size barracudas. Also, it blew steadily all that time— and I should add that Mr. Smith had stipulated he wanted a calm day. His family weren't "good sailors" he said, and he intimated that he was a "landlubber" himself.

It was blowing when we had our long-planned dinner together. All during that morbid meal I tried to explain that these "blank" periods happened—that our prospects for the next day were not just poor but almost hopeless—and that it would probably be pretty choppy, besides. Mr. Smith and his wife and son kept laughing off my statements. "Don't alibi," their attitude clearly said. "We've read your stories—in fact we've published scores of them. We *know* that everybody catches fish—*from reading your stories!*"

I pointed out, obliquely, that you couldn't have a fishing story without something being caught—and that the days— such as the days then current off Miami, when people trolled for twelve straight hours without a hit, didn't make good stories or articles. The Smiths just laughed harder.

I took my family home rather solemnly that breezy night and my folks shared my mood. If I had known anybody who practiced witchcraft I'd have paid them well, right then, to hex up even one minor fish. I slept very poorly that night.

Morning came. This unrested author rose and stared out the window. A bright sun shone. The palm fronds were limp.

Some fishing

It was a calm and lovely day. The worry over intense seasickness could be postponed, at least. I dressed, nervously. I put the
hamper of lunch Mrs. Wylie had prepared in my car. I drove to
the editor's hotel and collected him and his family. My daughter went along. But Mrs. Wylie, a woman of discretion, stayed
home because, I believe, she did not want to watch the spectacle of a beloved spouse suffering ever-greater agonies as the
day passed and nothing happened.

We proceeded to the dock, boarded the boat, went out
through the Government Cut and baits were put over. Other
boats, out earlier, reported via radiophone they had caught
nothing, seen nothing, so far. I tried to give interest to the trip
by pointing out landmarks on the Miami-Miami Beach skyline.
But the Smiths were, one and all, concentrating on the skipping
baits and on the rods they held. In about twenty minutes, the
Smith youngster yawned loudly—and my spirits sank further
as I wondered how he'd yawn after about eight empty *hours*.

Just then, Mrs. Smith had a strike. A nice one. She hung
and fought and we boated a dandy dolphin. All three Smiths
were rather pleased—more excited, I suspected, than they
revealed—but, on the other hand, they took the thing for
granted. My stories said such things happened. A few minutes
later, young Master Smith connected with a really powerful
'cuda. That was a scrap. The boy won it. And not ten minutes
after that, his dad and my editor hung *a sailfish!*

No fooling. Nobody—passenger, skipper or mate had even
seen a sailfish in the area for days. But Mr. Smith had one on.
He fought it rather dazedly but with a skill that grew under
the mate's coaching; he lost it, after many jumps, through no

fault of his own but simply because even the most adroit anglers do lose sailfish all the time, one way or another. The event, however, elated the editor. He got blood in his eye. And we began catching lots of fish, all game, all on light tackle—bonitas, more dolphin, albacore, other barracudas and kingfish. Lunch was a triumph. But listen to this:

In the middle of the afternoon another billfish rose—again, behind the editor's bait. He dropped back properly and struck. Out of the purple sea crashed *a big white marlin!* And, so help me, Mr. Smith caught it, after a Homeric battle of an hour or more!

When we and the other boats returned to the fishing pier that day it seemed as if we'd scoured the sea at the expense of everybody else. Nobody had half as many fish. Nobody had caught a marlin *for a month*. But I think the Smiths realized the enormity of their achievement only when, as the big catch was hung on the huge racks for photographing, a thousand pop-eyed bystanders crowded around to admire, praise, ask what that "gigantic" fish was—and to take hundreds of snapshots of their own.

I have never since had trouble in convincing that particular editor (and former bullhead man) that the Gulf Stream is a terrific place to fish. Indeed, I suspect he'd think our fishing was a lead-pipe-cinch, except for that white marlin. Nobody who, alone, unaided and single-handed has caught eight feet of white marlin in one piece *ever* thinks deep-sea fishing is exactly a cinch.

That was a day.

But, golly! What days *weren't?*

Some fishing

My daughter (the only chip off this block) didn't fish much until she was about sixteen. She stayed at school in the winter and up north in the summer amongst non-anglers. And then, when I did begin to take her out, she had rather poor luck. It lasted a year or so and until one hot and dazzling morning when, alongside the isle of Bimini, she hit into a wahoo bigger than herself. Karen—that's her name—caught the fish. It made quite a sensation on the Bimini docks: not even a local record, not by a long shot a world's record—just a beauty of a wahoo. But what father, what "old man" of any youngster, wouldn't give back to the sea, the lakes, the rivers and the brooks a hundred of his own best catches to be there when his kid made his, or her, first *really* good one?

Fine moments?

One of the most magnificent was a day when we *quit fishing just to watch the fish.* Ricky (that's Mrs. Wylie) and a friend and I were trolling over the "big reef" outside Key Largo, south and west of Miami, when the wind dropped and the clear, cerulean water turned as flat as a frozen pond. The sun was high and we could see down forty feet, fifty—a hundred, perhaps. We could see every house-sized coral escarpment and all the flaming sponges that grew on it. Every abyss was discernible. In the lunar submarinescape we could admire the giant purple "sea fans" and the yellow fans, which are smaller, as well as the colored millepores and all the particular corals: those that branch like staghorns, those that rise in leafy folds, like lettuce, those with convoluted domes, so rightly called "brain corals"—and all the rest.

Through this stone garden swam millions of fish and the

word "millions" is to be taken literally. They were of every size from inch-long, blue and orange Beau Gregories to ten-foot sharks that lay on white sand beds between coral crags and stared up with wondering but indifferent eyes at our ship's hull. They ranged through fish of the mackerel size. They included the incredibly bright-hued parrots. Sometimes schools of fish containing thousands of individuals—all of the same species and every one as bright as a Christmas-tree ball, with that same, near-incandescent color effect—drifted beneath us only to be followed by *another* school as big, of yet another species and another and another!

We watched the great groupers living down there—and the amberjacks; we saw, once or twice, sailfish moving in blue radiance through the enchantment. There were sea anemonies and sea worms with their flowerlike mouths agape. Spiny lobsters and octopi, too; shrimp and other crustacea. And it wasn't feeding time for anybody—or perhaps a truce had been declared. Anyhow, with almost Biblical tranquillity and assurance, the "lions" of the sea intermingled with its "lambs." The whole subsurface world of fish was displayed all afternoon—in a state of utter peace and of such beauty that I stumble in trying to convey any sense of the memory. It can't be said. It must be seen.

We didn't wet a line after that calm fell. We didn't need a glass bucket to see down. We just stretched out on the forward deck, or over the stern, and let the boat drift—passengers and mate and captain—all afternoon. We looked. It made another one of the greatest days I've ever had in fishing.

I have a record at my club—for a ninety-nine-pound white

marlin taken on twelve-thread line. Not a sensational catch and it stood quite a long time simply because none of my clubmates have happened to fish much, with that particular line, in white marlin waters. I remember the battle that fish put up —it was very exhilarating. I remember, too, my disappointment when the scales said, "99." "If that marlin," I kept thinking, "had only eaten one more mackerel that day, he'd have gone over a hundred."

But even more sharply I remember two other fish I *lost*. One was a tarpon. I hooked him from a dinghy while fishing down in the Keys with Leo Johnson. I was plug casting— using an ordinary black-bass rod and ordinary, twelve-pound-test Nylon line. Such gear is meant for such fish as the black bass mentioned earlier. But the tarpon I hung weighed, at Leo's best guess—and he's a conservative, experiencd guide —*a hundred pounds and somewhat more*. The total length of my line—incidentally—was a hundred yards. Figure it out for yourself:

If he has a mind to, a tarpon can run a thousand yards. Maybe ten thousand, for all I know. And a race horse would have trouble keeping up. But this guy—this aluminum-scaled monster—liked it where he was. All he *didn't* like was my plug in his jaws. So he spent the afternoon leaping, pinwheeling, shaking himself, tearing up the local bay. He never did put on a long, straight burst of speed—or I'd have lost him the minute he got one inch over a hundred yards away.

Sometimes, to be sure, he'd roll, grunt audibly and take off in a plodding manner, so that I gave line gradually until at last the fish was towing the two of us in the dinghy. But he'd tire of that—and jump again. We didn't count the times he fountained out and splashed back—a geyser of molten silver—a double explosion.

Perhaps he jumped, in the near-three hours I had him on —a hundred times. Maybe it was only fifty. Certainly he rolled part way out hundreds of times, for the water all around was from a mere three to six feet deep and he was always near the surface.

At long last, when he was so tired he could only thump his tail a bit and so move along on his side—all but belly up —I began to get him within range of Leo's reaching gaff. But the tiny reel "froze" at that moment—froze from the long strain of tight, wound line which finally bent its flanges against its sides so it could turn no more. The tarpon made a last try, when he saw the gaff, maybe twenty inches away. I couldn't give line from the stuck reel so—his last lunge paid off.

I darn near had him. I was within less than two feet—ten seconds of having him. At that date, he'd have been a world record for that tackle—though, as an IGFA official, I was and am not eligible for world records. Still, it would have been fun to have had an *unofficial* record even for a while. *Only* a while —because, since then, even *bigger* tarpon have been taken by *better* anglers on *identical tackle!*

Down there in the Keys, though, I feel sort of *even* with the tarpon. For there is a region along a flat called "Nine Mile Bank" which is, nowadays, referred to by Leo (and a few other guides) as "Wylie's Bight." Another day in another year—in a year before the wars—Leo and I fished there together and we saw, in the space of that day, only six tarpon. All six broke the surface. I cast at every whirl. Every time, I hooked the tarpon. *And I boated all six!* They ran from fifteen to thirty-seven pounds—not bad for bass tackle! In the local "books," nobody else has *ever* cast to, hooked *and caught* six tarpon in a row; and nobody's ever made a 100 per cent score for the day on even a lesser number of sighted tarpon! It's as near as I'll get, I guess, to making a legend—a little, local one. But—what a day *that* was!

Off and on, for many years, in such shallow, weedy, sandy or marly flats as bonefish feed on, I've tried to catch a permit. A permit is a kind of pompano which reaches about fifty pounds or thereabouts; it feeds on crabs and the like. It swims in on the flats so far its dorsal sticks out of water and, when it noses down to eat, out comes its tail. It is a very fast and powerful fish—some say, pound for pound, the fastest and most powerful. Years back, nobody had ever taken one on a plug. And in that era, one rainy, windy afternoon, I was casting over a "draw" on the flats when a big permit came out of the water and *caught my plug in the air!* I hooked the fool, too!

With the guide rowing manfully, we fought him over many draws and flats in the next hour. Permits, I learned then and there—when the water gets only inches deep—can turn on their sides and, looking like blue-and-gold flounders, swim just as fast and trickily as any upright bonefish! But this time, too, my reel froze. For a while I continued the fight by "stripping" line, as you do in trout and salmon fishing. Then—out of the roily, marly greenish-white depth of a "channel" came a black-tipped shark—after my hooked permit. The shark and I battled

220

each other for a long time—the permit was more on my side of it than on the shark's—but, in the end, the black-tip won. He grabbed and ate the biggish fish when I had it tired and very near the boat! . . . .

Forty years is a lot of years to have been fishing in. Each recollection of a "finest moment" casts up the memory of another. I could tell you, for example, about the time we hung "something" that fought so curiously and looked, in deep, dim silhouette, so odd—that nobody was ever sure it *was* a fish. What then? Search me: we lost him.

But I could tell how I took my father deep-sea fishing on Friday and Saturday (for the first time in his life) and how he came so close to catching a sailfish that, on *Sunday,* he rose before me and chartered the boat *again.* That was odd of father, you see, because he's a *Presbyterian minister.* In fact, he had already announced the church he'd attend that day. Well—we sailfished instead, preacher or no. And Dad got one! It's mounted, and on the wall in his study to this day.

There's some grumbling amongst some men about *women* and fishing. (My friend Chisie Farrington, famed angling wife of the celebrated Kipp, has written a swell book—for the ladies —on the subject.) But Mrs. Wylie has long since ended all debate, as far as I'm concerned. She is reputed amongst many male guides and even some anti-woman angling experts to be one of the fastest, smoothest light-tackle operators alive. And *that* gave both of us some unforgettable days—days like the early one (in her angling career) when she held my rod (four-ounce tip, six-thread line) so I could open a few cola bottles—

and raised, hung, fought and boated what proved to be, for many years, the heaviest sailfish ever taken by a woman on such light gear.

Or I could report how Harold Schmitt and I went "deep-trolling" (at several hundred feet), caught a big warsaw grouper—on heavy tackle—and, when we brought it in, posed it with Harold's young son and the lightest rod on board—*for a joke*. But some south Florida publicity man "released" the picture. We spent years afterward answering people from all U.S.A. who asked how such a *little* child caught such an *enormous* fish on such pitiful tackle!

And I remember one particular occasion when I took a newsreel man out fishing. I used very heavy tackle and promised I'd drag anything I hooked right up to the boat and then let off the pressure so the camerman could photograph the jumps —if any. I was hunting for sailfish. What I got was a very big bull dolphin. I reeled him to within *fifteen feet* of the stern. We swung the boat into the sun to make the light perfect. The camera was set up on the canopy. I eased off the drag and the dolphin jumped—more than eight feet high I believe—and eleven times. Then it collapsed—dead. I then looked up happily at the cameraman, sure he had the finest dolphin leaps on film. "Turn him loose again!" the man said amiably. "I wasn't set." No more fish that day, of course!

Forty years is a long, rich time to have fished in. But, as I say, fishermen are philosophers and they don't worry as other sportsmen do about age. For my part, I just wonder what I'll catch in the next forty years.